HAUNTED
HEREFORD

HAUNTED HEREFORD

David Phelps

The History Press

First published 2011

The History Press
The Mill, Brimscombe Port
Stroud, Gloucestershire, GL5 2QG
www.thehistorypress.co.uk

British Library Cataloguing in Publication Data.
A catalogue record for this book is available from the British Library.

ISBN 978 0 7524 6209 7
Typesetting and origination by The History Press
Printed in Great Britain
Manufacturing managed by Jellyfish Print Solutions Ltd

Contents

Acknowledgements

I would like to thank the people of Herefordshire, living and dead, who have helped me with this book, especially those who have told me stories. I hope that those stories appearing in this book will be sufficient payment but, if not, for the living I will stand them a pint in the hostelry of their choice; for the dead, I will light them a candle, in the church of theirs.

The details of medieval burial practices are based on research carried out by Claire Olszanska as part of the Cathedral Close Project.

Anyone who wishes to find out more about Hereford ghosts can do no better than going to the website www.haunted-hereford.co.uk, run by Natalie Lawrence, where they can also find out how to get involved in new investigations.

one

The County of Hereford: A Brief History

NOTHING ever happens in Herefordshire. Occasionally the council might find a priceless Neolithic trackway and build a road over it, sometimes they might decide to turn the essentially rural county into a suburb of Birmingham, but mostly the county does not make the news. This was not always the case.

Herefordshire was once border country, caught between the two warring kingdoms of Wales and England. In other words, it could be a difficult place to live – which might account for the many ghostly stories that come from this part of the world.

The old theory was that, after the Romans left, Saxon invaders pushed the aboriginal Welsh ever westward. This has not been supported by new DNA-based research, which seems to indicate that most people stayed where they were while aristocrats fought for power. A skeleton found in Wookey Hole, Somerset, carbon dated as 9,000 years old, was found (on DNA analysis) to have descendants still living locally.

It is now thought that as the ice retreated, 12,000 years ago, people started moving out of the refuges where they had survived the Ice Age. One group, based around the Pyrenees, slowly travelled around the North Atlantic coast, eventually arriving in the west of Britain. Another group, who had their refuge in the Caucasus region, travelled north up to Scandinavia and then down into the North Sea (which was then dry land) and on through England. The two groups met on the River Wye, and neither much liked the strange foreigners. So the Welsh/Saxon division is 10,000 years old, not 1,500 years, although it has been discovered that many people on what is now the English side of the border actually carry the DNA of their Pyrenean (Celtic) ancestry, borders and marriage always having been quite fluid.

It was previously thought that the centre of pre-Roman culture was centred around Salisbury Plain, Stonehenge, Avebury etc. but, over the last few years, this picture has changed as more research has been carried out in the area. This culminated in the discovery of the Rotherwas Ribbon in 2007. Just south of the city of Hereford, a serpentine path of deliberately fire-cracked stones was found, undulating from the River Wye up the nearby Dinedor Hill. Being only single stone depth, it was clearly not a path but what its purpose was is a mystery, best

Arthur's Cave; home to the first Herefordians. (© David Phelps, 2011)

put down to the great catch-all, some form of ritual. Dated to about 2000 BCE, this was the earliest use of fire-cracked stone in Europe and a completely unique discovery. The local stones were interspersed with pieces of quartz so, whatever its intended purpose, it must have shone in the sunlight and also, perhaps more importantly, in the moonlight, and be visible to anyone coming down the Wye (which was then the most usual form of long distance transport), so perhaps it was meant to portray the transforming power of fire and water.

Herefordshire also has the greatest concentration of Iron Age hill forts in the country, over thirty having been identified, indicating a sizeable prehistoric population of over 30,000. Given that the population of the county at the Domesday survey has been estimated as 25,000, this indicates a flourishing civilisation that was certainly more than subsistence farmers. The largest fort, at Credenhill, is larger than Maiden Castle in Dorset. These forts were thought to have been defensive structures but more recent archaeological evidence suggests that they were more often the home of the ruling elite, or possibly only used for special festivals or communal events – though some were heavily occupied at times. Given

Rotherwas Ribbon; since covered by a road. (© David Phelps, 2011)

that many were in use for 1,000 years, it is likely that their function changed over time.

There seems to be some confusion as to which tribal group ruled this area, with some scholars believing it was the Dobunni, whose capital was at Cirencester, while others put the case for the Silures of south-west Wales or the Cornovii of Shropshire. Some historians claim that it belonged to a completely different tribe, the name of which is not known to us. Probably this fertile ground was heavily disputed, and boundaries changed with alarming frequency.

It is tempting to see history as only really starting with the arrival of the Romans, because they brought writing with them and so could leave records. Yet, on a twenty-four hour time line, if the great ice retreated at midday and the first people returned at two o'clock in the afternoon, the Romans only arrived at ten o'clock at night. However, they made a big impact. The Dobunni tribe seemingly adapted to the new civilisation quite well, but the Silures set up an effective guerrilla war for many years. The biggest Roman settlement was at Kenchester, a few miles west of modern Hereford, just south of the largest hill fort in the county at Credenhill. One assumes that the people there were easily tempted off the hillside with the promise of warm baths and under-floor heating.

By tradition – and therefore not to be summarily dismissed – the Catuvellauni chief Caractacus, or Caradoc, driven from

Sutton Walls. This was once a royal hall. (© David Phelps, 2011)

his Hertfordshire homeland, made a last stand against the Romans at British Camp on the Malverns, before being driven off and making another last stand at Croft Ambrey, a large hill fort in the north of the county. He seems to have continued these last stands up through Shropshire and beyond, until being betrayed by the Brigantes of the north, who might have heard stories of his lack of success.

For the next 350 years the area was under the governance of Rome. People paid their taxes, grumbled and got on with life. The Romans brought a more urban way of living with them and there seem to have been three main settlements, at Kenchester (Magnis), Leintwardine (Bravonium) and Weston under Penyard (Ariconium). Kenchester was a thriving trading town, linked by fast roads to South Wales and the North. Given the problems with tribes to

the west, Leintwardine was an important military depot. In contrast, Weston under Penyard was an industrial centre, with many furnaces and iron forges.

As with all empires, eventually the tensions and disputes in Rome became too much, and its ability to control and collect taxes lessened. With pirates now ravaging the south coast, the local aristocrats brought in Saxon mercenaries to control the situation. The mercenaries, seeing that they could become richer by owning the land than by being paid to protect it, brought over their friends and relations and were able to conquer England, driving the Britons to the gloomy fastnesses of Wales.

Modern scholars are increasingly finding problems with this concept. While several mass burial pits have been found of decapitated male skeletons, dating to the Roman occupation and indicating the brutal way

Hereford Cathedral. (© David Phelps, 2011)

in which their empire was established, nothing like that has been found for this later period, either in Herefordshire or elsewhere. DNA analysis seems to suggest that while the ruling elite might have been forcibly changed, the common people just kept calm and carried on, much as the war-time government advised us to do in the event of German invasion. Intriguingly, modern place-name analysis also indicates that many Herefordshire appellations are much older than was once thought, and that the English/Welsh language boundary stretches as far east as Tarrington.

What does seem to have happened is that the whole country broke up into many petty kingdoms as competing war-lords sought to establish their power bases. Herefordshire may have been divided into at least two. In the south and west, the Kingdom of Ergyng (anglicised to Archenfield) derived from Ariconium. In the north-east, the Kingdom of the Magonsaete centred around Marden. Both Weston under Penyard and Marden are now small villages, although they were once home to kings – or at least people who called themselves kings.

Saxon defences that failed to stop the Welsh in 1055. (© David Phelps, 2011)

The people of Ergyng seem to have maintained their Christianity, established under the Romans, with wandering bishops who were later commemorated as saints, notably St Dyfrig (Dubricius) who, some say, crowned King Arthur. Eventually, the Bishopric of Hereford was established by Sir Geraint, one of the king's knights, in about 590 CE.

Nennius, one of the few historians of this period, also states that Anyr, son of Arthur, was killed by his father and buried at Wormelow Tump. Sadly, the Tump was destroyed as part of a road-widening scheme in the Victorian period.

Eventually, the independent kingdom of the Magonsaete was subsumed into the greater kingdom of Mercia. The greatest of these kings, Offa, was the first man who could legitimately call himself King of the English. His best-known monument is the eponymous Dyke, which probably defined the western boundary of his eighth-century kingdom.

Offa was also responsible for the foundation of Hereford Cathedral. In 794, he tricked King Ethelbert of the East Anglians (who had made the mistake of issuing coinage with his image instead of Offa's) to his hall at Sutton Walls, with the promise of marriage to his daughter Elfreda. Ethelbert was murdered in mysterious circumstances but, following miraculous signs showing where he had been hastily buried, Offa was forced to hold a more public burial in Hereford and, in penance, founded a cathedral on the site. So, a king of East Anglia became one of the patron saints of Hereford Cathedral.

Castle Green – all that is left of the castle. (© David Phelps, 2011)

With the Viking raids making life even more dangerous, Hereford was turned into a defensive burh, where the people could come in time of danger. Alfred the Great's daughter, Athelfreda, was stationed here when entrusted by her father with attacks on the Welsh. So Hereford's importance increased. By the time of Canute, at the beginning of the eleventh century, the area was referred to as Hereford's Shire.

The ascension of Edward the Confessor to the throne in 1035 caused further trouble. Edward had spent twenty-five years in exile in Normandy and was felt to favour these foreigners over local lords. They brought newfangled customs and defences, such as castles; the first ever on English soil is believed to have been built at Burghill. They also believed in fighting on horseback, which may have led to tragedy in 1055 when a horde of Welsh, Danish and disaffected Saxons attacked Hereford and the new earl, Ralph of Mantes, insisted that the local militia fight on horses. The resulting debacle near Whitecross led to the burning of the cathedral, the scattering of Ethelbert's relics and the Norman leader going down in history as Ralph the Timid, because of the speed with which he left the battlefield.

Roaring Meg; mortar that ended the siege of Goodrich. (© David Phelps, 2011)

After 1066, it was business as usual for the peasantry while their Saxon lords were replaced by Normans. For most, though, life probably took a turn for the worse as their new lords were keener than their predecessors on extracting their dues. William the Bastard wanted to subdue the Welsh, so he created a March – a border area between Wales and Hereford where Marcher lords could control all they could conquer.

So Hereford was in the front line – though, as well as a threat, it was also an opportunity. As a mark of the interest the king showed in the city, Henry I granted the bishop a lucrative fair in 1121, Richard I gave the citizens a charter in 1189, King John allowed them to form a Merchant Guild, and Henry III allowed them an annual three-day fair starting on St Denis's Day (9 October). In 1298, Edward I put a toll on woad, onions and garlic (probably for use in the dyeing trade), the proceeds being used to repair the city walls. This king's conquest of Wales made the castle less important but encouraged trade, especially in the cloth industry. Richard II allowed the city bailiff to call himself mayor. Victims of high politics, such as Hugh Despenser and Owen Tudor, found themselves brought to Hereford's High Town to be executed.

Hereford returned to the front line at the beginning of the fifteenth century with the revolt of Owen Glendower, and many Hereford men were slain at the Battle of Pilleth, just over the border. After his failure to create an independent state,

Owen disappeared, despite a high price on his head. Some think he evaded capture by constantly moving between Croft Castle, Kenchester Court and Monnington Straddle, whose lords his daughters had married.

In the War of the Roses, most of the local aristocracy favoured the Yorkist cause and one of the most decisive battles of the war was fought at Mortimer's Cross, in north-west Herefordshire, effectively establishing Edward IV on the throne.

With the ascent of the Tudors, Hereford fell into a long decline as it lost its strategic importance, from which, some say, it has still not recovered. Interesting times returned again with the Civil War in the middle of the seventeenth century.

Most wars have an economic component, and the end of the sixteenth and

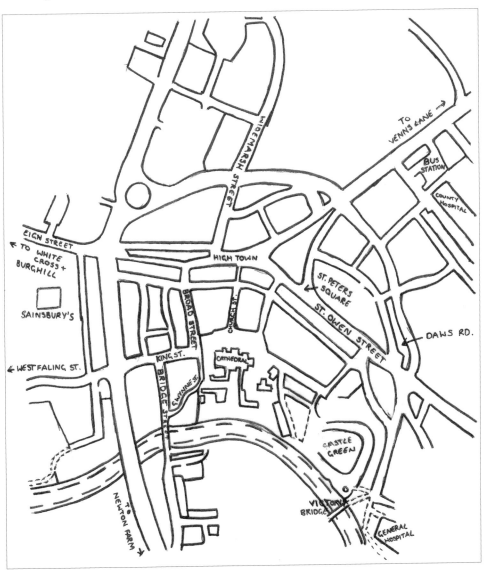

Hereford – with places mentioned in the text. (© Marina Phelps, 2011)

beginning of the seventeenth century were poor years for trade. Harvests had been bad and pestilence seemed a constant threat. The Ross area had been worse than decimated by plague in 1637. When the king's demands became too much for Parliament, Herefordshire's landed gentry were equally divided between Royalist and Parliamentarian, while the common people seem to have been much as they are today – moderately conservative, generally in favour of the status quo.

Herefordshire provided the king with important provisions and recruits but otherwise was not strategic, so no major battles were fought on her soil. The city of Hereford had a Royalist garrison that saw off a Scottish attack in 1645 (hence the city's coat of arms: English lions, surrounded by the saltire crosses) but fell to a surprise attack by Colonels Morgan and Birch the following year. Sir Harry Lingen and Sir Barnaby Scudamore escaped to Goodrich Castle. The 200-strong garrison were local men and made a good job of harassing the king's enemies. When Colonel Birch attacked the castle, Lingen seized his chance to dash back to Hereford. The general apathy of the population forced Lingen to retire to Goodrich, where Birch laid down a proper siege that lasted six weeks. After their surrender, Lingen and his men were allowed to march out of the castle with their arms, and a band playing the country air which was known forever after as Sir Harry Lingen's Fancy.

At the other end of the county and the other end of the political divide, Lady Brilliana Harley held Brampton Bryan Castle for the Parliamentary cause for a terrible seven weeks in 1643. Although the siege was lifted, Lady Brilliana died soon after, worn out by worry and the deprivations of the siege; the castle surrendered tamely the following year, whereupon it was slighted (had its defensive walls destroyed), as was the once mighty Wigmore Castle nearby, where the great Marcher family of the Mortimers had held court.

After the Restoration, Hereford slunk back into peaceful obscurity and relative poverty, its young people having to leave home if they wanted to find fame or fortune. Three who did so were Nell Gwyn – who found success on the stage and in Charles II's bed – and Sarah Siddons and David Garrick a century later. Given the slightly greater respectability of the Augustan stage, the latter two confined their careers to the theatre rather than having to take on a sideline.

The eighteenth century was particularly noted for its gloving trade, but economic change came slow and often too late. Herefordshire roads were nationally notorious, but turnpikes and tolls to improve matters were resisted. For much of the century some early adopters were agitating for a canal to join Hereford to Gloucester – but this was not popular with those to the east of the county who depended on the Severn for trade and did not want competition from the Wye. By the time the canal was being dug, railways were already spreading across the countryside and it never made a profit.

The great change that happened to the Herefordshire countryside was the Enclosure Act, which in Herefordshire occurred between 1779 and 1863. Field hedges were not a completely new invention and modern studies have indicated that, especially in the west of the county, some boundaries go back at least to medieval and possibly Celtic times. The idea of enclosure, however, was 'improvement' and the rationalisation of often dispersed holdings, but everywhere they worked in the favour of the bigger farmers and landholders, and smallholders and tenants might find themselves dispossessed and forced to become landless day labourers, or try their luck in the towns and coalfields. Hated hedges were grubbed up at night while underhand tactics were used by those in favour of enclosure, such as holding the meeting to decide on enclosure many miles from the village concerned. It is strange that we now regret the loss of many of these wildlife corridors, which are being destroyed by the descendants of the farmers who insisted on their necessity.

We often look back on the Victorian age as one of social stability, but in fact the Herefordshire countryside was rife with social protest, with potato rustling and cattle maiming the tools of those who felt a farmer had gone too far but found no other form of protest open to them.

In the twentieth century, Herefordshire again found itself in the front line. In the Great War of 1914-18 it lost 2,000 men, an almost exact decimation of the age group 18-45. In the Second World War, the munitions factory at Rotherwas suffered an air raid in 1942 that failed to damage the factory but destroyed a nearby house, killing the inhabitants.

Herefordshire briefly lost its identity when it was amalgamated with Worcester in 1974. This act was repealed in 1998, but wise old heads are shaken and some say that things have never been the same since.

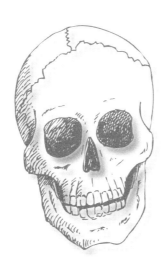

two

Ghosts and Their Relations

WHEN our earliest ancestors buried their dead, they included in the grave goods that might be useful to the deceased. While this might be considered a nice mourning gesture, most people have taken it to mean a belief in the after-life. If there is an after-life, it is natural to assume that the dead can, in some way, interact with the living. It is tempting to think that belief in ghosts is one of the first things that made us human.

The oldest known ghost story appears in one of our earliest tales, *Gilgamesh*, written in about 2000 BCE, but based on much earlier oral traditions.

There are marked differences in our view of ghosts through the centuries. In Anglo-Saxon times people, as indicated from the literary sources that have survived, seemed principally concerned with being harmed by the dead that would not rest, and put in place gruesome burial customs to prevent this from happening. Up until 1823, the law required suicides to be staked and buried beneath roads rather than in consecrated ground. Latterly this was meant as a punishment but the original custom, which also applied to serious criminals, was to prevent them from walking. In the medieval period

there was a plague of tormented souls who had become grotesque animals; this was taken as a warning of the horrors of Purgatory. They could find peace through posthumous absolution.

After the Reformation, when Purgatory was no longer fashionable, learned men redefined ghosts as devils in disguise. But this view was not popular and it was taken that, if there was an afterlife, there had to be ghosts. Stories of ghosts that had been seen by aristocrats, gentry and other people who could be trusted became common. In an earlier period, ghosts were held up as a warning to people to mend their ways, but now it appeared as if they had motives of their own – to denounce their murderer, warn a friend of approaching death, or make good some evil they had done in their life. There were even wraiths that came to the living to announce their own death. Instead of charging around the place making a nuisance of themselves, as medieval spectres mostly seem to have done, these ghosts often behaved with great dignity. Those noisy spirits that we might now classify as poltergeists were accepted as demons rather than the unquiet dead.

In the eighteenth century – the time of the Enlightenment – belief in ghosts, once shared across the social spectrum, was held by the elite to be stupid superstition, fit only for the poor and the simple.

A hundred years later, as many local customs and beliefs were being lost in rapid industrialisation, folklore collectors still found widespread belief in ghosts. While folklorists were more interested in legends, this period also saw the advent of psychical researchers and spiritualists, who were much more interested in personal reminiscence. Increasing attempts were made to put psychical research on a scientific basis, and the idea was put forward that ghosts were not the dead themselves but a re-playing of some past incident so emotionally powerful that the event had become imprinted on its surroundings. This led to the idea that there were some people more 'psychic' than others, who were therefore more likely to feel this atmosphere. Ghosts became more terrifying as writers such as Dickens, Le Fanu, Blackwood and M.R. James emphasised their evil, horrific side. This historical process has, according to a recent book by historian Shane McCorristine (*see* Bibliography), 'produced the thousands of ghost and haunted house stories for which England is so well known, and which has given it one of the highest densities of ghost-associated locations in the western world.'

In the last few years a new theory has been put forward as to why some places are more haunted than others. This concerns how we experience infrasonic sound waves. Under the right atmospheric conditions, these can produce a feeling of dread or even hallucinations.

How our ancestors felt about ghosts was mediated by religion. As this influence is no longer as powerful or uniform, it is difficult to be concise about how we experience spirits. The folklorist Jeremy Harte has pointed out that ghosts only started taking on the appearance of the distant, rather than very recent, past at the end of the nineteenth century and, 'nobody saw the ghosts of Roman soldiers … until the arrival of mass education taught the public that there had been such things.' He also points to the proliferation of ghosts from popular eras, such as pre-Reformation monks and Civil War soldiers, rather than less fashionable periods. What is certain is that ghosts have not gone away. A study in 1990 found that roughly a quarter of Americans believed that the spirits of dead people can come back; this belief was higher among the well educated than those without a college education. A report in *The Times* newspaper in 2009, based on recent research, stated that four in ten Britons believe in ghosts.

My own interest in ghosts comes from my love of stories and, while there are innumerable instances around the county of spectres being seen for no known reason, I have only included them in this book if there is a good story attached to their haunting. Any apparitions who feel aggrieved by their omission are advised to contact my publishers for inclusion in any subsequent edition.

Rather worryingly for people who might be tempted to go looking for them, in Herefordshire ghost sightings have generally meant bad luck. Often those who see them do not live for long afterwards!

three

The City of Hereford

BRIDGE STREET

The Black Lion pub is the most haunted building in Hereford, with fourteen different ghosts being identified as haunting the place. The building dates from the mid-sixteenth century so has had some time to collect them. The epicentre for the hauntings is the upstairs Painted Room, not generally open to the public, that contains fascinating wall paintings but also unexplained noises and footsteps. It is believed that the building was once an orphanage and that one of the ghosts is that of a little girl that staff call Alice. More creepy is the ghost of a man in a hat, who has been known to tap customers on the shoulder.

An earlier inn near this spot had a more sinister reputation. Back in the thirteenth century, two merchants came to Hereford. One had been here many times before and had business contacts that he could stay with, but his friend was making his first visit and so had to find an inn. Staying in a medieval inn was not the enjoyable experience that we tend to expect now. Tired after their journey, the two merchants went into the first inn they came to, by the bridge.

The Black Lion – the most haunted building in Hereford. (© David Phelps, 2011)

The landlord here was a great bear of a man, surly and taciturn, but that was par for the course for medieval landlords, who had to keep their rough clientele in order. Seeing his friend taken care of, the other merchant went to the town house where he would spend the night. He was well entertained and then shown to a private bedchamber. He felt pity for his friend, who was probably having to share a bed – and possibly with more than human companions.

In the middle of the night the merchant woke up, disturbed by a dream. He had dreamt that his fellow traveller had visited and pleaded with him to come to his aid, because he was being attacked by the landlord. The merchant was greatly perturbed by the dream, but his bed was warm and the street outside was quiet so he soon slipped back into sleep.

But the man had a second dream in which his friend appeared to him again, reproaching him and asking him to at least come and see that he was properly buried because the landlord was planning to dispose of him in a very un-Christian way. Now, terribly worried by this confirmation of his original dream, the merchant got dressed and went out into the night to ascertain the truth. He immediately ran into the town watch, whose job was to detain anyone found in the streets after dark without good reason. He could well have spent the night in the small prison beside the castle but he managed to persuade the man to wake up his host, who vouchsafed his good character.

Reluctantly, the watch agreed to accompany him to the inn. When they turned the corner into Bridge Street, they saw the figure of the landlord walking towards the bridge carrying something over his shoulder. They let out a cry and the man dropped his burden and tried to run off, but was quickly caught. The bundle was found to be the body of the second merchant and, although his friend had not prevented the murder, at least he could give his friend a Christian burial and see that the landlord faced justice.

BROAD STREET

At the corner of this street and West Street is the fine Georgian building of the Queen's Arms. The bar of this pub is haunted by the ghost of a man dressed in Saxon clothes. This seems strange unless you know that this was the boundary of the old Saxon settlement. People have speculated that this might be an unfortunate defender of the town during the unsuccessful defence of 1055, who has still not come to terms with his death.

The large hotel that dominates this street, the Green Dragon, is an old coaching inn, where coaches collected the mail on a daily basis. Here, in the 1830s, when fear of body snatchers was rife, staff became suspicious of a hamper that had been left there for delivery to an address in London. They looked inside and were horrified to find the body of an old man, clearly destined for dissection. Despite this, it is the third floor that guests and staff find the most eerie, feeling that there is a strange presence about it, though none can define what it is.

Also on this street is Hereford Museum. One of its strangest exhibits is a curse doll, believed to have been made in the late nineteenth century at East Street, just around the corner from the museum. It looks like a nice, child's toy, but a paper found pinned to it tells a different story:

Mary Ann Ward
I act this spell upon you from my holl [*sic*] heart wishing you to never rest nor eat nor sleep the rest part of your life I hope

The Green Dragon – the scene of a body snatching. (© David Phelps, 2011)

your flesh will waste away and I hope you will never spend another penny I ought to have Wishing this from my whole heart.

The reasons for the curse and its effect on the unfortunate Mary Ann Ward are not known, but it gives us an authentic voice from this period and shows what people wished upon each other when feelings ran high.

Also in the museum and also from the nineteenth century is a small block of wood shaped like a coffin, which some people believe is haunted. Inside is a human figure, pinned down in the coffin by a nail. It was found at a house in Woolhope and, as soon as it was discovered, mysterious things began to happen. A woman living at the house was almost killed when an entire window fell on her from three storeys up and her daughter fell ill. Blaming the discovery of the coffin for these occurrences, the woman donated it to the museum. While considering what to do with it the curator kept the coffin in her office. Then her husband was involved in a serious car accident. The coffin was quickly moved to a display case. No further spooky goings on have been recorded.

BURGHILL

The A4110 was once a major coaching road going up to Shrewsbury and Knighton. On this road there was a cottage with an elm tree. Beside this tree was sometimes seen the ghost of a pig, which would shuffle around the tree as if chained to it, before backing into the darkness under the tree and disappearing. Sadly, the tree fell victim to Dutch elm disease in the 1970s and the ghostly pig was lost with it.

THE BUS STATION

This was the site of the old workhouse, though nothing now remains of it except the building on the left of Union Street (now occupied by travel agents) and a toilet block. This was the Master's residence. The last master was so upset by the ending of the workhouse system that he hanged himself. Some people have reported something unpleasant around the toilet area, and it is not a place that most people would wish to loiter.

Hereford Cathedral. (© David Phelps, 2011)

THE CATHEDRAL

The cathedral is dedicated to St Mary the Virgin and St Ethelbert the King. Ethelbert was a Saxon king of East Anglia who was murdered by King Offa of Mercia in 794 CE. The body was buried at what was then the monastery of Fernlea, the old name for Hereford. So many miracles were attributed to it that, with the aid of gifts from pilgrims, a magnificent cathedral was built.

Nearby is St Ethelbert's Well, the site of a miraculous spring that ushered forth at the spot after the future saint's body rested there overnight before being buried.

Bus station – the last remains of Hereford Workhouse. (© David Phelps, 2011)

The original cathedral was burnt down in 1055 in what is often called a Welsh raid, but in fact had quite a few English in the party. Edward the Confessor had spent his early life in Normandy and was felt by many Saxon nobles to unfairly favour Normans. Earl Aelfgar of Mercia was one of those Saxons, and he felt slighted that a Norman called Ralph had been made Earl of Hereford. He joined the Welsh prince Gruffydd in an attack on Hereford, which was met by Ralph at a site possibly near White Cross. Unfortunately the Norman Ralph, used to fighting on horseback, insisted that the Saxons, trained to fight on foot, did as well. The result was chaos and the survivors, led by a man who would now forever be known as Ralph the Timid, rode for Worcester. A couple of monks were not so lucky and were cut down in front of the High Altar, which was where the Lady Chapel now stands. Figures dressed in white have been seen here and, it is claimed, they are the ghosts of the unfortunate monks, vainly trying to protect the relics of St Ethelbert, which were lost in the raid.

One of the rare instances of haunting by the undead outside Eastern Europe occurred in the Cathedral Close, at the time that Gilbert Foliot was bishop. One of the corpses in the graveyard took to rising from its grave at night and visiting the inhabitants of the Close. Those who heard its voice outside their door soon sickened and were dead within three days. Fortunately, one of its victims was a knight called Sir William Laudun, who, instead of shrinking in fear, drew his sword and decapitated the thing. Hereford has not been troubled by the living dead since.

The cathedral suffered badly from having lost the body of its patron saint, Ethelbert. Fortunately help was at hand. Thomas Cantilupe was elected bishop in 1275 by the canons of the cathedral. He was learned and pious, but also a very cantankerous man who seemed to fall out with almost everybody. He fell out with the powerful Earl of Gloucester, and then he went too far and quarrelled with the Archbishop of Canterbury. So heated did this later dispute become that the Archbishop excommunicated Thomas, forcing him to make the difficult journey to see the Pope in an attempt to have the excommunication lifted.

It proved a death sentence because Bishop Thomas died before he could see the Pope. As was the custom in such situations, his body was boiled and the bones brought back to Hereford. Then strange things started to happen. People started to visit the tomb in the Lady Chapel and pray, as they would to a saint, the bones began to bleed in the presence of the Earl of Gloucester and, on Palm Sunday 1287, a madwoman, Edith Oldecriste, was cured by being brought to the tomb. It was attracting so many visitors that the new bishop, Richard Swinfield, who had been Thomas' secretary, ordered it to be moved to a more prominent position in the North Transept. The event was considered so momentous that the king, Edward I, was there in person. But then the masons found that the tomb was too heavy for them to move. Fortunately two young novice monks, innocent and without sin, stepped forward and were able to carry it all the way to its present position.

Immediately, other miracles began to be reported, including people being brought back to life after drowning and, in one case, after being hanged. In 1320 Bishop Thomas was declared a saint, the only one ever to have died excommunicate. Linked in many people's minds with St Thomas of Canterbury, his shrine became the second most visited by pilgrims after that of the

The Kerry Arms, haunted by Old Hoskins. (© David Phelps, 2011)

Archbishop. As late as 1610, his bones were carried around the city at night to protect the people from an outbreak of plague. However, thirty years later his bones suffered the same fate as those of St Ethelbert when they were dispersed by iconoclasts.

In 1290, a demon was found in the choir stalls after matins, dressed in the robes of a canon. Another canon, asking him why he was still sitting there, got no answer and realised that this was no brother monk but an evil spirit. He bade him, in the name of Christ and Thomas de Cantilupe, not to stir from that place. He fetched help and the monks beat the creature, put him in fetters and threw him into the cathedral prison. His eventual fate is not recorded.

Visitors to the cathedral often listen entranced to organ music and assume that it is the cathedral organist practicing. Ninety-nine times out of a hundred this is the case, but the organ has also been known to play when there is no one in the organ loft. These supernatural recitals are attributed to John Bull, who was organist here in the early part of the seventeenth century.

In the 1780s, Mr Hoskins, a long-serving verger, became frail and was retired. He died soon afterwards but his token (the old Herefordshire name for a ghost) was still seen going about his duties in the cathedral. This became a *cause célèbre*, with people coming from miles around in the hope of seeing the ghost, so much so that it was interfering with divine service. Therefore it was decided to exorcise the ghost, an act that was carried out by twelve local clergymen; the spirit was confined in a silver snuff box and buried in the city ditch at Byster's Gate. Canon Underwood, one of the officiating clergy, is reported to have come home after the event with his shirt wringing wet with sweat – at least according to his servant girl.

How well a job they did is open to question because, a few years later, the West Front of the cathedral collapsed, taking the spire on the East Tower with it, and many people said that was Old Hoskins' revenge. Quite a few people coming out of the Kerry Arms, which now stands on the site of Byster's Gate, have reported being

Church Street –
Lichfield Vaults is on the left.
(© David Phelps, 2011)

Hereford Cathedral, the West
Front. Old Hoskins' revenge?
(© David Phelps, 2011)

passed by an old man dressed in black; many people think that the old Gate should not have been taken down, because it must have disturbed Old Hoskins.

The West Front of the cathedral, restored after the collapse of the tower in 1789 (some people, who do not like the restoration, say this is the true revenge of Old Hoskins), is often used by picnickers, and recently married couples who want a nice backdrop to their photos. What they may not realise is that it is also the site of several plague pits, discovered in the excavations for the building of the new Mappa Mundi building in 1993. The Black Death hit Hereford in the autumn of 1348 and archaeologists think about 300 bodies were buried at this site. It has been estimated by the Hereford archaeologist Ron Shoesmith that Hereford's population fell from 3,000 to just 1,000.

CHURCH STEET

The Lichfield Vaults is haunted by a mischievous spirit that moves barrels and hides objects, even making beer mats fly in the air. It is probably more of a poltergeist than an actual spirit; some people find its antics endearing while others are freaked out by it.

COUNTY HOSPITAL

This site was, until the 1930s, the city slaughterhouse, which stood where the front entrance and car park are now. Muffled voices have been heard at this spot but, on investigation, no one has been there. Dore, Kenwater and Lugg wards seem to have a particular reputation, with some staff refusing to go past them alone at nights. Patients seem to be mostly unaffected but staff, resting during a night shift, have found blankets ripped off them as they lay in bed. In the building of the new hospital, four workmen were killed in an accident at the spot where Lugg ward now stands.

DAWS ROAD

Belle Vue Terrace, on this road, has a fearsome reputation among some previous tenants. They report a feeling of oppression haunting the house, and items vanishing only to re-appear in unusual places. Worryingly, the front door has, on several occasions, been found wide open in the morning, although securely locked the night before. Several people have reported waking in the early hours of the morning to the sound of children running up and down the stairs, although there were no children in the house.

EIGN STREET

The Horse & Groom pub has a very lively ghost who delights in patting ladies' bottoms. A heavy object has also been heard being dragged

County hospital, site of the old slaughterhouse. (© David Phelps, 2011)

across a room upstairs. Invariably, when investigated, the room is found to be empty.

GENERAL HOSPITAL

This former hospital by the river, now flats, is haunted by a Grey Lady. She is believed to be the ghost of a nurse who had an affair with a married doctor. Finally understanding that the man was never going to leave his wife, she committed suicide. However, she has not lost her sense of duty. A nurse fell asleep at her desk when on night duty, until woken by a returning colleague. Feeling guilty, she went to check on the patients on her ward and was surprised when one thanked her for retrieving some blankets that had fallen off his bed. Several other patients also said they had been helped by a nurse during the period the night nurse was asleep. Her colleague was adamant that she had not done it and no other member of staff claimed to have visited the ward.

GWYNNE STREET

A ghostly female figure seen walking along this road near the cathedral has, inevitably, been identified as Nell Gwyn, who, tradition states, was born on this street around 1650 when it was known as Pipe Lane and something of a slum. With the same inevitability, the ghost of a cavalier-like figure seen riding down the street has been identified as none other than Charles II, though what this pair are doing haunting this street – which the king never visited and Nell did not return to once her mother had taken her to London as a toddler – is a mystery.

General hospital, haunted by a grey lady. (© David Phelps, 2011)

HIGH TOWN

The most prominent building on the square is the Old House, now standing alone but once part of a string of half-timbered buildings called Butcher's Row. The upstairs rooms have a particularly eerie feel and staff have reported that the curtains of the four-poster bed in the main bedroom have closed of their own accord, and the bed in the smaller bedroom has unmade itself.

Across the square is an apparently modern shop selling computer games, though the shell of this building actually dates to the eighteenth century. It also seems particularly troubled by spirits, with objects going missing and then being found in unexpected places, and noises and loud footsteps

Old House, the last survivor of Butcher's Row. (© David Phelps, 2011)

upstairs when no one is up there. The story is that a man hanged himself in one of the upstairs rooms, which may account for the noises. Additionally, the building was once used as an orphanage, and a young girl who died here also haunts the place.

Another shop nearby is haunted by a monk. Several members of staff have seen this ghost, who has been nicknamed Charlie. He is especially prone to knocking objects off shelves in the stockroom. In the basement are the remains of tunnels (tradition links them to the cathedral) that may have something to do with Charlie. He is generally described as a pleasant ghost, so one assumes that whatever Charlie was doing in the tunnels, it was a pleasant mission.

At the west end of the square is a small black and white house, squashed up against

High Town – the house that moved. (© David Phelps, 2011)

its neighbours. This house was once moved further east while the current modern development that now obscures it was built. In the eighteenth century this was an apothecary's shop. In those unregulated days it was all too easy for ingredients to be put in the wrong bottles and become mixed up, especially as apothecaries then made up their own potions from raw materials that they had gathered. Whether by accident or design (there was talk on both sides) the apothecary's apprentice ate a pill that should have been harmless but contained poison and he died. Filled with remorse, his master went into a deep depression from which he did not recover. For many years his restless soul could be heard pacing in the shop but, after the move, he was heard no more.

Life for most people living in medieval Hereford was quite hard. One night, a freeholder of High Town was tossing and turning so much in his bed that his wife asked him what was the matter.

'Wife, I have calculated the income that we need to get through the year and I believe we have enough for the year except one day. Now I cannot rest for thinking how we shall get through that day.'

The whole night through he worried but then, with the approach of dawn, he hit upon a method of how to overcome this problem. 'I have it,' he said, waking up his wife to tell her the good news. 'I'll pretend that I am dead for a day and you'll put me in the hall and cover me, and that day I won't eat anything because I am dead and you and the household won't eat anything because of your grief, and so we will have enough for the rest of the year.'

So the plan was put into action and, as the household arose, the wife let out cries and lamentations that her good husband had died in the night. The 'corpse' was placed in the hall with a sheet over it and no food was prepared. But what the man had forgotten was that servants talked and soon word of his death started to spread, eventually reaching the clergy of the cathedral. Now, at this time, the priests of the cathedral had the monopoly of burying people for miles around and, because burials cost money, made a good income out of it. When word of the death reached them, one of their number was deputed to visit the family and make the arrangements.

After he had said a Paternoster over the body, he asked for some food as it was approaching the accustomed hour of his dinner. The 'widow' excused herself, saying that, in their great sadness, nothing had been prepared.

'Nay, good woman, we must eat. It is eating that distinguishes the living from the dead,' said the priest, and was so insistent about the bother he had gone to that the woman felt she could not arouse his suspicions, so she fetched him a good meal.

Hearing the sounds of guzzling and realising that his plans had been thwarted, the householder raised his head. The priest, seeing this and assuming that some evil spirit had taken hold of the body, seized an axe that was lying nearby and dealt the man several mighty blows.

The woman screamed, 'You have killed my husband!'

'No, I have driven a devil from your husband's body who was intent on turning it into a ghost, but now it is ready to be put in consecrated ground.' And so it was.

Death was an ever-present feature of medieval Hereford. When death was imminent, the most important thing to do was send immediately for a priest, because it was believed that it was at the moment of death that a person's salvation or damnation was decided. The priest, once warned, would make his way to the stricken person with the sacrament; a server walked ahead of him with a lighted candle (to represent Christ's presence) and a hand bell to warn people in the street to kneel or pray in reverence to the sacrament. On the return journey the candle would be extinguished, to show that Christ was no longer present, the sacrament having been eaten by the dying person.

On arrival, the priest would say prayers and take confession. At the point of death the bell would be rung to remind the faithful to pray for the soul of the departed. The body was then laid out immediately after death, as a final check that death had occurred. A night watch would take place while the body remained in the house – not in the same room, although a lighted candle would be kept in the room, placed in the centre of a plate of salt, both to keep away evil spirits. The naked body was placed in a shroud, men in hair-sheet and women in linen. Afterwards, the body was taken to the cathedral, placed before the altar and surrounded with candles while services, including a Requiem Mass, were said.

Coffins were re-usable and owned by the parish, and were only a means of getting the corpse to the grave. This was done in a procession, grandeur dependent on wealth, but commonly headed by a man ringing a bell, followed by a candle bearer. Behind him came a cross bearer and then another candle bearer; then would come two robed priests walking backwards, one carrying a book of prayers and the other sprinkling holy water on the road in front of the coffin. They were followed by the four bearers of the coffin, which was draped in black cloth. This was followed by another candle bearer and then the mourners. Although burial was not considered as vital as the last rites to ensure salvation, the body still had to be buried properly to enable physical resurrection on

Judgement Day. The body was lowered into the grave without the coffin. Graves were aligned west to east, with the body facing the east to await Christ's coming, although priests would face the east, so they could attend to their flock when the great day arrived. For most classes of people graves were either unmarked or might have had a simple wooden cross. In this hierarchical society rank was maintained even in death, with higher status bodies nearer the altar (either within the cathedral or to the east), poorer people placed to the west, and the people the priests were not too sure about (such as suicides and the excommunicated) placed to the north.

Despite following all of these procedures, one unfortunate woman found that her husband came back to her the night after his burial, and attempted to get into bed with her. For three nights this happened, each time the woman having to fight the ghost off. So, the woman persuaded her friends and neighbours to keep watch with her. When her husband came back the next night he was repelled by the large body of people, but then went to bother his brothers instead. In the end the entire community was forced to set up an extra night watch, each house forced to keep a vigil – but then the man took to appearing in the daytime as well. Now the people sent a deputation to the bishop to ask for his help. The bishop was amazed by these goings-on but was advised by some of his canons that the usual remedy in such a case was for the body to be dug up and cremated. Only then would the people be pacified.

But the bishop found the idea of cremation abhorrent. Instead, he ordered that a scroll of absolution should be prepared and placed in the man's coffin. When this was done, all haunting and trouble ceased.

Lawyers, in the Middle Ages, were treated with suspicion, as they have been in every age. They were neither lords, who could offer protection and largesse, nor one of the people. It was assumed that they were selfish and just out for themselves.

One day, one such lawyer was on his way from his lodgings (at the Booth Hall in High Town) heading towards the castle where he had ordered a man to be detained for debt. As he came out into the street, he found a man dressed entirely in black standing there as if waiting for him. They became engaged in conversation and it soon dawned on the lawyer that this was the Devil he was talking to. This did not greatly alarm him because they had many devious tricks and stratagems to discuss.

They were walking down a narrow lane leading to the cathedral when they met a man leading a pig on a rope. The pig was intent on his own business and was going this way and that, driving the man to distraction. Eventually the man could take no more of it. 'The Devil take you!' he cried out in his annoyance. The lawyer looked at the Devil. 'Hear that my friend? That pig is given to you, go ahead and take him.' But the Devil shook his head. 'That's not the way it works. That man did not say that with all his heart, therefore I cannot take it.'

They continued on further when they came upon a mother and child, the child crying loudly and refusing to be pacified. 'The Devil take you!' cried the mother in irritation. 'Why do you annoy me so with your crying?'

'See that,' said the lawyer, 'you have gained another soul. Take the child, he is yours.'

'Ah, good sir, she did not give him to me with her whole heart, that is just the way people speak when they are angry.'

At last they came to the castle and the dark cell where the debtor was imprisoned.

When the wretch saw the lawyer who had caused his misfortune he cried out in a loud voice, 'You! Do you come to torment me more? May the Devil take you!'

Hearing this, the Devil laughed and turned to the lawyer. 'There, that man has spoken from the depth of his heart and therefore you are mine.' The Devil took hold of the lawyer, there was a clap of thunder and a flash of sulphurous smoke, and the lawyer was seen no more in the city, although whether that is also true of the Devil I am not so sure.

KING STREET

Early one morning, a passer-by was going past the Spread Eagle pub when she saw what she described as a woman dressed in an old-fashioned way glaring at her from a top window. Thinking the woman was in trouble she alerted the landlord, but the room was found to be empty when searched.

Just up the road, the Orange Tree pub is haunted by a nun looking for her baby. It is said that she had an affair with a monk from the nearby Greyfriar's Abbey but, inevitably, it did not end well. The nun was parted from both monk and baby, and died of grief. She was buried in the old St Nicholas' graveyard, which was then on this spot. When the church was moved across the road to its present spot, in the nineteenth century, all bodies were supposed to have been dug up and re-buried in newly consecrated ground but, in the 1990s, when repairs were being made to the road outside the pub, the diggers discovered an old crypt. Since that time the nun has been seen more often, wandering about the pub and nearby offices as if still searching for her child.

The Orange Tree, haunted by a sad nun. (© David Phelps, 2011)

NEWTON FARM

This post-war suburb to the south of Hereford has had an unusual number of poltergeist manifestations reported to the housing department and the Anglican South Wye team ministry. Reports have included moving furniture in empty rooms, objects being thrown – sometimes directly at people – and strange knockings and other unexplained noises. Many modern supernatural researchers associate poltergeists with troubled people, or adolescents having difficulty making the transition from childhood to adulthood. The fact that the area is home to a large number of young families may therefore explain the high incidence of these noisy ghosts here.

SAINSBURY'S

The modern supermarket was built on the site of the former Barton railway station, which was mainly a goods yard but also formerly dealt with passengers. It seems to be haunted by a passenger who never completed her journey. The manager arrived very early one morning and saw an old lady waving at him from across the car park. Thinking it was an early customer, he went over to her but, before he could get near, she disappeared. She has also been glimpsed in other parts of the store and most people who have sensed her describe her as a nice presence.

ST OWEN'S STREET

A house on this road, once a brewery, is haunted by the shy ghost of a young girl with long, dark hair, who has been glimpsed but who vanishes if anyone tries to look directly at her. A workman in the cellar put his screwdriver down and, when he came to retrieve it, found it had moved to the other side of the room, despite there being no one else around.

ST PETER'S CHURCH

The money for founding the original church was given by one of William

Newton Farm, a housing estate which was probably once a farm, has a high level of poltergeist activity. (© David Phelps, 2011)

the Conqueror's barons, Walter de Lacy, but he never saw it completed. Going up the tower one cold December to see how the building was proceeding, he slipped on some ice and fell to his death. In December 1926, two policemen saw a hooded figure approaching the church door and disappearing. Thinking to catch a burglar, the policemen searched the area thoroughly but no one was found. Other sightings of this phantom have been reported, usually in the same month, wearing what people assume is a monk's habit but which might also be the travelling gear of the eleventh century.

The Shire Hall is still used as a court, as it has been since it was built. The site was also the city gaol and, when public executions were considered a good form of entertainment and instruction, hangings took place outside, where the war memorial now stands. There is a rumour that one of the prison governors used to take the bodies of the hanged and feed them to his pigs.

Some people have seen a dark apparition in the jury wait-ing room, while others have smelt cigar smoke, even though the whole building is a non-smoking zone. The ghost of a little girl has also been seen playing outside the front door, apparently quite happily.

VENN'S LANE

While working on this book, someone told me an unusual tale of what he thought was a poltergeist but which might have been something more personal. He was taking part in an art club that meets at St Barnabas' Church hall when his tube of Titanium White, without which any painter knows you cannot work, went missing. The other painters swore they had not taken it and a search failed to find it. He would have thought no more about it had it not been for the fact that, a few weeks before, his car had been written off in an accident. Preparing the log book to send back to the DVLA, he went to check the address of the garage where the car was. On coming back he found parts of the document missing. It was only some days later that he found it, lying under the window of his late wife's bedroom, although no one else had been in the house in that time. Perhaps not so much a poltergeist as a personal tease.

VICTORIA BRIDGE

This suspension bridge, known locally as the Vicky Bridge, has provided a pedestrian crossing over the River Wye for over 100 years but, long before it was built, the site, in the shadow of Hereford Castle, was popular with the city's washer women for laundering clothes. This was a grim profes-

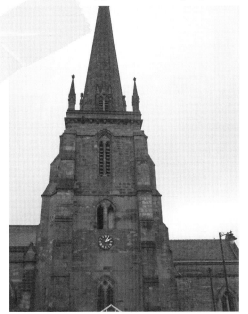

St Peter's. The tower from which Hugh de Lacy fell.
(© David Phelps, 2011)

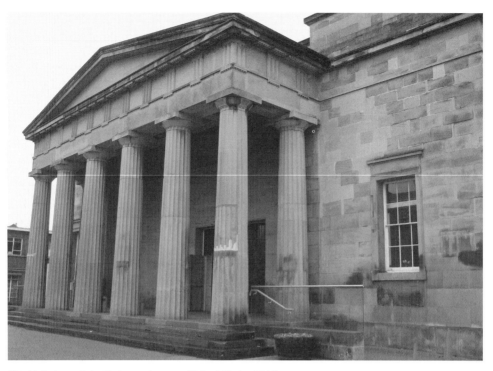

Shire Hall, where a little girl plays on the steps. (© David Phelps, 2011)

sion because, not only did you spend many hours up to your knees in the cold river, but the coarse soap blistered your arms, hands and legs. Still, it had the advantage of being a communal activity, where the gossip could be shared and the characters of the people whose linen they were washing frankly discussed.

One evening, one washerwoman found herself alone on the riverbank, the others having finished for the day. Hurrying to complete her task she was careless and, too late, noticed that her expensive block of white soap had been caught by the river and was being carried away. She rushed to retrieve it but in her haste stepped into deep water and was swept off by the current.

She thrashed about but there was no one around to hear her cries and all the thrashing only took her further from the bank. Then she felt herself grabbed by strong arms. For a moment she thought she was saved but then she realised that she was being taken not to the bank, but farther along the river.

The rest of her journey passed almost like a dream but, coming to her senses, she found herself in a huge underground cavern populated by creatures that looked almost human but were much thinner and taller than her own folk. The male creature who had taken her now approached, bowed low, and explained to her that he was the lord of the people she could see. His wife had recently given birth to a child and they prized a human nurse above all others. He promised her that she would be well taken care of and, after the child was weaned, she would be returned to her own people. She would be brought her own food, and he warned her that on no account must she eat any of the food that his people ate.

Not having much choice in the matter, she set to work as a nursemaid and found

Victoria Bridge, scene of a fairy abduction. (© David Phelps, 2011)

that being nurse to a fairy child was much easier than being a washer woman in the world of men. One day, as she was taking the remains of some eel pie (a delicacy that her mistress was particularly fond of) back to the kitchens, something went into her right eye and, without thinking, her hand went up to it, and she accidentally rubbed some of the grease from the eel pie into her eye.

After about a year, the baby now weaned, she was thanked for her services and taken back to the riverbank where she had fallen in. Her reappearance caused a great stir in the city, for seven human years had passed since her disappearance and it had been assumed that she had drowned, and her husband had remarried. It was naturally assumed that she was a ghost and many people were forever fearful of her. However, the local gentry were quite excited about having their clothes washed by someone who was either a ghost or else had been nurse to a fairy, so she prospered.

One Wednesday, it being market day, she was in what is now Castle Street, where the market then was, with a spare silver coin, looking at the stalls and wondering what to buy, when she suddenly caught sight of her former master, dressed in black, going from stall to stall, picking up whatever he chose and putting it in a sack without any of the stallholders trying to stop him. Without thinking, she went up to him and enquired how his wife and child were faring. The creature gave a start of astonishment. 'Which eye do you see me with?' he said, and she pointed to her right eye in which she had smeared the grease from the eel pie.

Immediately, his arm was up and he dug his finger into the woman's eye, blinding it. From that moment on she saw no more fairies and only half saw the things of this world.

White cross, erected by Bishop Charlton.
(© David Phelps, 2011)

WESTFALING STREET

This suburban street is reputed to be haunted by the ghost of a monk who appears suddenly in the street, walks along it for a little while and then disappears. Speculators, especially those who do not like the ever greater spread of the city into previously green fields, believe that this might be the spirit of a monk or medieval traveller buried around this spot, whose now restless spirit was disturbed by the building.

THE WHITE CROSS

Originally erected by a bishop of Hereford to mark deliverance from the Black Death, and recently restored after a drunk driver failed to notice it, the present cross probably replaces a simpler cross put up in the time of plague. Farmers, protected by the sign of the cross, could bring food for the beleaguered population of the city, who would pay for it by dropping a coin into a bowl of holy water or vinegar. Bishop Charlton, a few years before the plague, was warned to erect the cross when, returning from his palace at Stretton Sugwas, he was greeted by a peel of bells when he reached this spot but no human ringer was found in the bell loft.

At the beginning of the nineteenth century the site was haunted by the ghost of Old Taylor, who used to farm 'Morning Pits' Farm but had moved a monument in life and subsequently could not rest. One stormy night, Denis the Liar ran into the pub near the cross, which was then called the Nag's Head and is now unimaginatively called The Monument. (Its previous name, The Foxhunter, commemorated a local showjumper who won a gold medal at the Helsinki Olympics.) Denis claimed to have seen Old Taylor's ghost and had promised to meet the spectre at the Morning Pits at midnight. Everyone laughed and thought it was just another of his stories but, at midnight, it was found that Denis was missing.

When he returned he was in a shocking state. He said that he had not meant to keep his promise but somehow had found himself at the farm at the appointed time. Old Taylor was waiting. 'Follow me,' it had said, and Denis did. They came to two immense stones. 'Take up those stones!' said Taylor.

'I can't,' replied Denis.

'You can. Try!'

Denis found that he could tilt them easily. 'Now come with me and place them where I show you.' Denis did so. 'Now,' said old Taylor, 'Never tell anyone about what you have seen here this night. Lie down on your face and, as you value your life, don't attempt to look either way until you hear music, and then get away as fast as you can.'

It seemed a long time before Denis heard what he was waiting for and, instead of waiting to listen, he high-tailed it away from the place.

Many people said he was a fool to tell the story. Certainly he was a changed man after his ordeal and died soon afterwards.

WIDEMARSH STREET

The pub currently called JD'S has a haunted ladies' toilet. People have heard rustling and movement in the cubicle next to them but, on leaving, have found it empty. The upstairs kitchens also give patrons an unpleasant feeling and the sensation of being watched. Once, an unknown figure was caught on CCTV in the kitchen when none of the staff were upstairs. Lights have switched themselves on and off without human agency. The building is on the site of Widemarsh Gate, part of the old city walls. Perhaps one of the old watchmen does not approve of the modern goings on.

The multi-storey car park on this road was once the site of the Garrick Theatre, built in honour of one of Hereford's most famous sons, the actor David Garrick. Here, in April 1916, a concert was held to raise money for comforts for the Herefordshire Regiment, then serving in Gallipoli. The performers were forty local children, dressed as Eskimos, ice maidens and snow-balls, in costumes made out of cotton wool, who delighted the audience with mock snowball fights and other wintery pageants.

As the final curtain fell and the girls trooped off the stage, somehow one of the children's cotton wool costumes caught fire, which spread to others. There was a cry of 'Fire!' and chaos in the audience, as some tried to get to the exits and mothers tried to get to the stage.

News of the disaster spread and crowds flocked to Widemarsh Street – some were merely onlookers but some were distraught parents, anxious for news of their children. Eight young girls died in one of the greatest tragedies to rock the city that century.

Over time the horror was forgotten and the theatre was torn down, but the occasional shopper, returning to their car, has glimpsed something white moving out of the corner of their eye. When they look there is nothing there. A seagull? Or perhaps a ghostly reminder of when laughter turned to screams of pain within seconds.

The Oxford Arms dates back to the seventeenth century but is haunted by a much earlier ghost; a monk appears in the bar, walking towards the front window – at least the upper part of him does, his feet are beneath the floor. In the cellar is a blocked-off tunnel that was thought to lead to the nearby Blackfriars Monastery. Hereford monks seemed to have liked the subterranean life. The building was used as a bakery before it became a pub and is also home to the ghost of a small girl, thought to be a victim of a fire – a too regular danger of early bakeries.

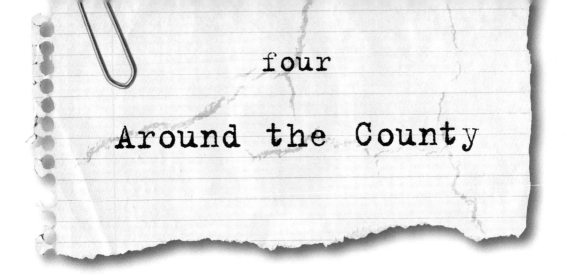

four

Around the County

ABBEY DORE

Nanny Gunter lived at the Cockyard, near Abbey Dore. She was a reputed witch and dark tales were told about her, claiming that she had murdered her children and buried them in a nearby wood, and that she terrified the schoolmaster and children at the Abbey Dore school house by walking around it late at night, thumping her stick and making the windows shake and the chairs, plates and dishes rattle.

There is still a stretch of road here called Nanny Gunter's Pitch, which some local people try to avoid as it gives them a bad feeling when they travel along it, even in a car.

Abbey Dore. Storytelling in the village hall, once the school. (© David Phelps, 2011)

ACONBURY

Roger de Clifford was not an evil man, but as a knight he had to do things that did not rest easily on his conscience. When he felt his death approaching, he went to the nuns of Aconbury convent and promised them a large sum of money if they allowed him to be buried within the precincts and said a daily mass for his soul in perpetuity. All went well until the Reformation, when such masses were abolished. Then the ghost of Sir Roger began terrorising the parishioners and disrupting the services. Eventually, the vicar decided to perform an exorcism and confined the spirit in a bottle. Then he buried it beneath the tomb in the church wall, so that it was neither in the church nor out of it, to prevent the ghost from walking again.

However, confining an unquiet spirit to a bottle may not have been the most practical of solutions; bottles have a habit of breaking, especially when placed in cold church walls. In the nineteenth century, the ghost started bothering churchgoers once again. It was said that, if it appeared, the ghost would reach out its hand to try and touch its victim. If it succeeded, then that unfortunate would be dead within the year.

Aconbury church is now unused and kept locked, so few visit Sir Roger's tomb. It is still possible to visit the over-grown churchyard, although such an excursion is best done in a group. If alone, the mind starts playing tricks on itself, and the wind rustling leaves and shaking the grass will soon make you want to leave.

Near St Anne's Well, not far from the church, is a spring that is haunted by two lovers. The young girl, believing her young man to be untrue, killed him at the spot where they would often meet. Later, on finding that her suspicions had been false, she died of remorse. The two spirits still meet at their special spot, trying to achieve the happiness in death that was denied to them in life.

Aconbury church, haunted by Roger de Clifford. (© David Phelps, 2011)

ACTON BEAUCHAMP

The first wife of Hodges, the blacksmith of Acton Cross, died, leaving two young children. The blacksmith quickly married again, to provide a mother for the children, but the stepmother had seen too many pantomimes and ill-treated the children.

The first wife's spirit came back to comfort them, appearing by their beds, but they were not frightened of her because she was dressed in her normal clothes rather than a shroud. However, the stepmother was angry and insisted that the parson perform an exorcism; the spirit was confined to a matchbox and dropped into Amstell Pond. The pond has since been drained and there have been no reports of the spirit returning; her family are presumably now grown up.

AVENBURY

This church, ruined at the time of writing but with plans to restore it, has the reputation of being one of the most haunted buildings in Herefordshire. The restoration work has been plagued by vandalism, delaying the project. Some attribute this to bored local youths but others say there is a more supernatural explanation.

Many years ago, the organist here had a n'er-do-well brother who kept plaguing him for money. Finally putting his foot down, the organist refused. Incensed, the other brother attacked and killed him, and then escaped to America; he was not brought to justice.

Nothing upsets a spirit more than its murder not being avenged. From that moment, the villagers of Avenbury would often hear organ music coming from the church, but, on going there, would find the church deserted. Even after the church fell

into ruin, the sound of a long-lost organ could – and still can – occasionally be heard in the fields around.

The bell of the church was also heard to toll when there could be no human ringer. Then people noticed that, soon after such an event, the incumbent vicar died. Perhaps it was no surprise that, when the church was closed, the bell was sent a long way away, to St Andrews by the Wardrobe in the City of London. Even in its new home the bell was heard to ring as late as the 1990s but, fortunately, both the vicars of St Andrews and Bromyard remained in good health.

The church was also haunted by the ghost of a Nicholas Vaughan, who had burned down the palace of the bishop of Hereford in the Middle Ages. You are unlikely to see this ghost as an exorcism was performed on it, with the requisite twelve priests with twelve candles, and the spirit was confined to a silver box and thrown into the River Frome, to remain there for 1,000 years. But the time is nearly up, as the local saying goes.

AYLTON

In 1855, the tenants of Aylton Court were the Foulger family. Emma, just fourteen, was running down the stairs to greet her brother, who had just returned from his first shoot, when the gun went off accidentally, killing her almost instantly.

The distress of her family did not end there. A few days after her burial, a farm labourer was going to work past the graveyard early one morning when he saw Emma's grave had been opened and the body gone, presumably taken by resurrectionists for dissection in the medical schools of London.

Not surprisingly, her ghost has been seen in the hall of the Court and the church-

Emma's empty grave at Aylton church. (© David Phelps, 2011)

yard, although, instead of anger and distress, anyone seeing the ghost feels a sense of peace. Emma seems to be one of the few forgiving ghosts.

AYMESTREY

In the Middle Ages, a local man was led astray by a Pwcha, a mischievous spirit. He spent a terrible night in Pokehouse Wood. After that he set aside a portion of land, the rent of which was to pay for a man to ring a bell in the church at dusk every night to guide any traveller that had suffered the same fate. Sadly the rent became too small to attract a ringer and the practice ceased, so watch out if you are in that vicinity late at night.

BRAMPTON BRYAN

After the siege of the castle in the Civil War, the death of his wife and the victory of Cromwell, Sir Edward Harley set about rebuilding his estate. However, he refused to sign Charles I's death warrant and became estranged from Cromwell in consequence.

He had nearly completed the repairs when, on the night of 3 September 1658,

a great storm devastated the area and undid many of the repairs. A few days later, news came from London that Oliver Cromwell had died on that same night. Sir Edward attributed the storm to the Devil dragging Cromwell to hell, coming through Brampton Bryan to spite him. On that date every year, the Devil is still said to ride through the Park.

Nearby is 'Laugh Lady Dingle', with a spring that sometimes gushes out fiercely and sometimes issues forth with a gentle gurgling sound, depending on the mood of the spirit of the stream. It is believed that if a gift of a pin is dropped into the pool and bubbles come off it then the wish made will be granted, especially if the wish concerns love.

BRINSOP

The church here is dedicated to St George and there is a very good reason for it. The Dragon's Well is in Duck's Pool Meadow, on the south side of the church. On the north side is a field called 'Lower Stanks' and it was here, according to the locals, that St George killed the dragon.

BROMYARD

As my grandmother lay dying she asked my mother to take off her wedding ring, because it was a sin to bury gold. A farmhouse near Bromyard was haunted by the spirits of two sisters so badly that no servant would stay there. Finally, a girl from Hereford was found who was prepared to put up with the furniture clattering and shaking every night.

She was alone in the kitchen one night when the two spirits came to her and told her to go with them to the cellar. When there they asked her to move a heavy stone, and beneath it was an earthenware pan filled with gold. The ladies warned the girl that she could have it but she must give the present tenant his fair share. Then they disappeared and no further disturbance occurred at the farm.

Stories are important, especially when it comes to ghosts, and it is a tragedy when one is lost or just not known in the first place. Such is the case with the phantom that haunts the Falcon Inn in Bromyard. He was first seen in 1964 and, because he was in contemporary dress, at first no one recognised him for what he was. But then it was noticed that he kept disappearing and reappearing, and his true nature was realised. His usual habit was to pace down the corridor crying, 'Annie, where is Annie?' Unfortunately no one could work out who this Annie was and the ghost seems doomed to continue his haunting until his question can be answered.

BURRINGTON

Wild Edric, the Saxon thane who married a fairy, had land here. So successful was his revolt against William the Bastard that the fearful Normans believed he commanded the Wild Hunt, ghosts that ride through the sky on stormy nights predicting disaster to any who hear them (hence his reputation for haunting). One night, when he was returning late from hunting accompanied only by a boy, he lost his way. About midnight, wandering in search of the path, he came upon a house on the edge of a wood. Attracted by the light of the house, he looked in and saw a band of noblewomen – the most beautiful he had seen and clad in the finest linen, taller and statelier than human women. Edric noticed one of their number whose beauty far exceeded the others. At the sight of her Edric was wounded in the heart.

He went around the house and, finding the door, rushed in and seized the lady whom he desired. He was immediately resisted by the others, who attempted to hold him back, and he only escaped with the greatest of difficulty and the help of the boy, although he bore on his feet and shins the marks of the teeth and nails of the other women.

He carried the woman back to his hall and took his pleasure with her for three days and nights; she passively submitted to his love. Then, on the fourth day, she said, 'My dearest, you shall be safe and joyful, and you will prosper, until the time when you reproach me because of my sisters. From that time onwards your happiness will disappear.'

Edric promised to be firm and faithful in his love and solemnly married the lady. William the Bastard, hearing of this marvel and wishing to test its truth, summoned the pair to his court in London. There the woman's great beauty was the chief proof of her fairy nature.

Years passed and the couple had a son, whom they named Aelfnoth, but then, returning from hunting one evening, Edric

Callow Farm, where dark deeds were done. (© David Phelps, 2011)

could not find his wife and called for her. After a long delay she arrived. He looked angrily at her and said, 'Did your sisters keep you?' The rest of his angry words were spoken to empty air for she disappeared at the mention of the word 'sisters'. Then Edric regretted his grave mistake and went to the very place where he had made her captive, but, for all his crying and lamenting, he was never able to win her back and the rest of his life was passed in great sorrow.

Their son, Aelfnoth, lived a long and saintly life. In old age he fell victim to the palsy and his friends suggested that he travel to Rome, to pray to St Peter and St Paul. 'Why should I do that,' said Aelfnoth, 'when I live in the diocese of Hereford and can go to the altar of St Ethelbert and pray for a cure there?' He did so and was cured. In thanksgiving he left many of his manors to Hereford Cathedral and was buried within its precincts, so, there is the son of a fairy buried in Hereford Cathedral.

CALLOW

Callow Farm, near the church, was once a coaching inn. Eventually it was noted that several lone travellers who had stayed at the inn never made it to their destination. The landlord was interrogated and confessed to murdering the missing men and carrying their corpses, with the help of an accomplice, across two fields to another house that he owned. The men were hanged at Callow Tump, near the Belmont Road bridge, and the house, where up to thirty bodies were discovered, was burnt down. Motorists on the A49 have occasionally contacted police to report a house on fire at the spot where the house once stood. Two phantom figures carrying a heavy burden have also been glimpsed in the fields by the church. Callow Hill still takes a terrible toll of road casualties, but if this is due to speed or to people distracted by a burning house it is impossible to say.

Canon Pyon; one of Robin Hood's Butts. (© David Phelps, 2011)

Prior's Court, in the same village, is haunted by a cavalier of the seventeenth-century civil war. Lord Leven's Scottish troops passed this way en route to the siege of Hereford and acquired an evil reputation. It is said that they captured this unfortunate enemy of theirs and walled him up alive in the Court.

CANON PYON

There are two strangely conical wooded hills near the village called Robin Hood's Butts. This is how they were created: the Devil took a dislike to the people of Hereford over their saintly ways so he got two big sacks of earth from the side of Dinmore Hill and set off to Hereford to bury the place.

However, the people of Hereford, being saintly, heard of his evil plan and one of the canons of the cathedral set out to meet him, disguised as a cobbler, with many pairs of shoes hanging from his back. Meeting the Devil at Canon Pyon, he engaged the old 'un in conversation and the Devil asked him how far it was to Hereford. 'Man,' said the canon, 'If you were to wear out all the shoes on my back you still wouldn't reach it.' Hearing this, the Devil thought better of his task and emptied the sacks on the spot. A few years later, Robin Hood passed this way and his friend Little John bet him that he could not stand on one of the hills and shoot an arrow onto the other. Robin won that bet and they have been known as Robin Hood's Butts ever since.

CHECKLEY

As part of the research for this book, I was in communication with a lady who was formerly a cook at the Yew Tree Inn. She was making chutney in the downstairs kitchen one day – something she had not done before – and was following the printed recipe very closely. She read at one point that she needed four tablespoons of salt, and was just going to add this when a voice shouted down to her, 'You need four teaspoons, not tablespoons.'

She thanked the voice, which she thought belonged to a friend who was also a cook there, and carried on with her work. Having successfully finished her task she thanked her friend, who denied having called to her and, anyway, had never made chutney herself so had no idea how much salt might be needed. Later she was told of an old woman who had died in the building back in the 1960s. Apparently, she had been a great chutney maker.

The same respondent remembers showing a new member of staff around. When they reached that kitchen, all the utensils started to shake on their hooks, making a terrifying sound. The tour was cut short.

CLIFFORD

A man living in Wales was in an ale house when he saw a man in black ride up. Intrigued, the man went out to meet him. The rider bowed and held out a tankard to him, but something warned the man not to take it. The figure in black smiled and toasted the fellow's health. Then, in a hollow voice, he commanded the man to go to Clifford Castle, take some money that was hidden there and throw it into the river. 'Do this, I charge thee, or thou shalt have no rest!'

Feeling he had little choice, the man carried out his task and saw no more of the ghost. He never spoke of the events until he was on his death-bed and became concerned that he might have committed a sin by conversing with a ghost. The priest set his mind at rest and so the story was preserved for posterity.

Clodock, haunted by a black dog. (© David Phelps, 2011)

CLODOCK

The church here is a fine place to visit and many people enjoy walking along the quiet lane from here to Longtown. If you do, be careful, as a phantom black dog has been known to follow walkers as well as vehicles along the lane, until it reaches a certain spot and then disappears.

COLWALL

Colwall Stones stands at roughly the centre of this spread out village. It is a square block of limestone believed to have once formed a wayside cross. Alternatively, it may have been thrown at Colwall by the Devil or by a giant who lived in a cave up in the Malverns. One day he looked down and saw his wife talking with a man on Colwall Green. Giants being supremely jealous, he supposed it to be her lover and he picked up the stone and threw it at her, killing her instantly.

Barton Court and Hope End were owned at the end of the eighteenth century by Henry Lambert, who had only one daughter, Sarah. She was targeted by a penniless Yorkshire baronet, Sir Henry Tempest. He disguised himself as an old gypsy woman and accosted Sarah on Colwall Green, offering to tell her fortune. 'She' said that if Sarah was to go to Colwall church the next day, she would meet the man she would marry. Of course, the man she met there was Sir Henry Tempest.

Soon he had persuaded her to elope. Henry sent his coach for her but the coachman, who did not know the area, went to Blackmore Pitch, east of the Malverns, rather than Chance's Pitch (now on the A449)

Malvern Hills, from where the giant threw the stone. (© David Phelps, 2011)

where Sarah was waiting. The poor girl wandered for three hours in pouring rain until the coachman found her at Barton Holloway, a narrow, sunken road nearby.

What Sir Henry did to the coachman is not recorded. A ghostly coach is still said to haunt Chance's Pitch, although this is usually thought to relate to an earlier coaching accident. Certainly the omens were not good for this marriage. As soon as the couple returned, Sir Henry threw Sarah's father out of Hope End, since this had been left to Sarah by her mother, and he was forced to go and live at the smaller Barton Court.

Soon husband and wife quarrelled and Tempest threw Sarah out as well, but Henry Lambert refused to take her in. Forced to live with relatives, it was only after her death that she could return to the area, and her ghost has been seen at Barton Court and Barton Holloway. So regular were sightings that the sons of the owners in the mid-nineteenth century took to using the ghost as target practice.

The story must have been well known to the poet Elizabeth Barrett Browning, who lived at Hope End as a child, although that did not seem to have put her off elopement – fortunately with happier results.

CRASWELL

A labourer, who worked at Black Hill Farm, was sitting by the fire in his cottage one evening when he saw a white face at the window. 'Who's there?' he called out, but received no answer. This happened over several nights and the man came to the conclusion that this must be a ghost. So, the next night, when the face appeared he used the correct form of address, 'In the name of God, who art thou?'

The figure then came into the cottage, got hold of him and took him flying many miles until they came to a wall. The man was told to take out some stones and he found a box. Then, carrying the box, he was taken on a further long journey until they came to a pool, into which the spirit made the man throw the box. Then the ghost disappeared but the unfortunate man had to make his own way home. He arrived back at dawn, shoeless and his clothes in rags. He was never the same again and died soon after.

Craswell, where the labourer met the ghostly lady. (© David Phelps, 2011)

When the owners of Abbey Farm in the 1920s were repairing the oven in the farm-house, they decided to use the old oven in the abbey ruins in the meantime. After setting the fire they returned to the farm-house, but went back to the ruins when they thought it would be warm enough. They saw the figures of a man and a woman standing at the fire, with their hands raised to it, warming themselves. They were dressed in old-fashioned clothes and their bodies were without substance. The owners returned to the farmhouse, all thoughts of a warm meal forgotten.

As with most abbey, priory and mon-astery ruins, spectral monkish shapes have also been glimpsed in the ruins.

CREDENHILL

The Court once had what can only be called a family tree – a great elm, called the Prophet Elm, because it would drop off a limb when any member of the family who owned the Court died.

CROFT

The castle, now owned by the National Trust, was the ancestral home of the Croft family. In the Middle Ages this was a border castle and the Crofts were a turbulent border family. Richard Croft fought at the nearby Battle of Mortimer's Cross, a deci-sive battle in the War of the Roses. Some say that it was he who advised the future Edward IV as to the best tactical disposition of his forces in countryside that Richard Croft knew well.

The building we see today is a much more tranquil place, having been remodelled by Sir James Croft in the mid-eighteenth century. Sir James seems to be a more peaceable man than his ancestors,

Mortimer's Cross. A peaceful scene, once a battlefield. (© David Phelps, 2011)

A servant was in the hallway when he thought he heard a coach drawing up on the gravel drive outside. Opening the door to find out who it was, he found the drive completely empty. He kept quiet about it until the same thing happened to another servant. Then it kept on happening, and some even heard the crack of the driver's whip as the coach came up the drive. Eventually it got so bad that the old house had to be demolished.

Croft Castle, whose long-dead owner checks on building work. (© David Phelps, 2011)

because it is his benevolent ghost that people claim to have seen. The ghost is only seen when building work is being carried out at the castle. It will seem to be inspecting the changes and then slowly dissolve away, presumably accepting any alterations that bring the building up to date – in the way that he did when alive.

DILWYN

The Homme was a grand house that used to stand to the south-west of the village. A servant died in mysterious circumstances but the owner insisted it was due to natural causes. This was accepted by the powers that be, though the other servants thought differently. Then the noises started.

DORSTONE

It is believed that, at Halloween, the Devil, standing in the pulpit, reads out the names of all those of the parish who will die in the coming year.

One year, a local man called Jack France decided to test this out after spending the evening at the nearby Pandy Inn. On reaching the church door, he heard his own name being read out. Now a good sight more sober he made his way home and mended his ways – but still was dead by Christmas.

Up on the hill above the village lies Arthur's Stone, a Neolithic burial chamber. The stones, once covered, are now exposed and some people who have made the journey to see them have experienced a strange humming that gradually increases in volume and then stops suddenly. The burial chamber got its name because local people believed that it was here that

'Old Arthur' fought a desperate single combat with another king before eventually breaking his back and burying him under the stones. Other stories claim that it was a giant that Arthur fought here and, in proof, people will show you stones – under the hedge and to the left if you are approaching from the Bredwardine direction – which still bear the marks of the giant's fall. Trained archaeologists laughed when they heard this tale, because they knew this structure was much older than the time of Arthur, even if he had existed, which they doubted. But those who have followed them into the profession are not so ready to ridicule the story. It is understood about those times, the so-called Dark Ages, that a spot like this would have been chosen as a focal point for fairs and get-togethers, and a place that rival chieftains, whatever their names, might choose for single combat. Perhaps a local tale hides a long-forgotten piece of history.

EARDISLAND

A restless spirit was confined in a silver box and laid under the bridge over the River Arrow, to stay there for 1,000 years. But the time is nearly up and horses are reported to bolt when going over this bridge, cars break down and pedestrians are overcome by a feeling of dread.

EARDISLEY

Parton Cross is haunted by the Cwn Annwn, the dogs of hell – black mastiffs which roam the air searching for souls to drag to hell, so to hear that ghostly baying would truly be a horrific experience. Coincidentally, the manor was owned in the medieval period by the Baskerville family.

Eardisley, haunted by the dogs of hell. (© David Phelps, 2011)

Arthur's Stone, where King Arthur fought a giant. (© David Phelps, 2011)

Eardisland Bridge – under which a spirit is confined. (© David Phelps, 2011)

EASTNOR

The fine gothic castle was only built in 1812, replacing an earlier, but draughtier, castle at nearby Bronsil, the ruins of which can still be seen. Here a huge raven, which local people assumed must be a spirit from hell, could always be seen near the moat. It was said to guard a treasure hidden under the island on which the castle had been built. The original owners were the Beauchamp family who, from these 'humble' beginnings, went on to become Earls of Warwick. But the treasure could only be found if the rightful heir should approach the raven, who would recognise him if he was carrying the bones of the original Lord Beauchamp.

It was said that, in the time of the first Queen Elizabeth, a Mr Gabriel Reede inherited the castle through the female line, but was troubled by a restless spirit that walked at night. He was advised by the wisest man in the kingdom, Master Allen of Gloucester Hall, Oxford, to procure a bone of the first Lord Beauchamp and to keep it in a cedar box in the castle. This silenced the ghost. When the Reede family moved to New Court in Lugwardine, they took care to take the box with them, just to be on the safe side.

EWYAS HAROLD

The Temple Bar pub has a rich history. As its name suggests, it was once used as a petty session court. When a new landlord took over he was anxious to discover all he could about the place, and was glad when the district nurse called into the bar and was happy to regale him with local stories. Later, when he described the storyteller to other regulars, he was told that the woman he had talked to had died some years before. The ghost of a boy also haunts the pub, although some say it is the ghost of a jockey, of small stature, who was murdered in the building. Also here is the ghost of a dog, which brushes against the legs of customers.

EYE

Just north of Leominster is the imposing mansion of Berrington Hall, built around 1780 and now owned by the National Trust. One might expect such a building to be home to any amount of Georgian ghosts but its principal haunting seems to belong to the twentieth century. During the Second World War the house was used as a hospital, and soldiers recovering from their wounds were the first to report this ghost, that of an infantryman in contemporary uniform. The ghost does not seem alarmed but just goes about his business quietly, so that many of the soldiers must have seen him without realising what he was. The sightings continued long after all the other men in uniform had left. It is presumed that this is the spirit of one of the soldiers who died of his wounds here and is now quite content to remain. The National Trust has now restored the house and the grounds, originally laid out by Capability Brown, to their original 1780s appearance, so this ghost must feel that he has actually gone back in time.

FOWNHOPE

The Green Man pub has a ghost with the disconcerting habit of locking people in rooms – or even out of the building. The pub was used as a petty session court in the eighteenth century and a spectral figure of

The Green Man, where a hanged man seeks revenge. (© David Phelps, 2011)

a man in shackles has been seen, so perhaps the presence is just getting his own back. Bedroom 3 seems particularly haunted, with some people feeling it unnaturally cold, and a mirror there moves of its own accord.

GARWAY

It is said that there will always be nine witches from the bottom of Orcop to the end of Garway Hill and, for one man of the village back in the Middle Ages, it was just as well that that was so.

This man, a member of the Mynors family, whose ancestor had come over to England in the household of William the Bastard himself, lost his wife, whom he loved dearly. He mourned for her deeply for three years, even though all his friends told him that he should get over it and start looking for another wife. At last, one of

these friends took pity on him and told him to consult one of the old ladies on Garway Hill and see if there was anything she could do to get him out of his misery.

He climbed up the hill to consult the woman, not without a little trepidation. When he got to her hut and told her of his problem, she looked very deeply into his eyes as if looking for something.

'You did right to consult me,' she said. 'Because your wife is not dead even though you buried her. That which you buried was but a simulacrum made by the fairies. Your real wife has been taken by them.' The man did not know whether to be glad or despair but the old woman assured him that there was one way of getting her back, as long as he obeyed her instructions to the letter.

The next May Day Eve he waited, hidden, by the spring beside Garway church. As dusk approached, he heard the most beautiful music that he had ever heard in his life and saw a shadowy band

Garway Spring. Beautiful and mysterious figures have been seen here. (© David Phelps, 2011)

of dancers appear almost as if out of the mist by the spring. Whether they were ghosts or the fairy folk he had no idea, but he recognised one of the figures as that of his dead wife. Before he could doubt himself, he rushed forward and grabbed hold of her, picked her up and then ran as fast as he could up the hill away from the church. It sounded as if the very hounds of hell were chasing him, and the load that he carried burned as if it was the coals of hell, but he neither looked back nor dropped his burden. Even when his wife pleaded with him to let her go he said nothing, but just kept right on running.

Eventually, as his legs and his heart felt they could go no further, the moon came out from behind the clouds and all sound of pursuit died away – and there was his own dear wife in his arms looking as if she had just woken up from a terrible dream.

The couple later had many children and grandchildren, and their descendants lived for a long time in the area; for all I know they are living there still, and all of them are known as 'the sons of the dead woman'.

If you go to Garway now you can follow the man's desperate race up the hill from the church to the village. Afterwards, you will probably want to refresh yourself at the local pub, which is called the Moon.

GOODRICH

Alice Birch, niece of the Parliamentarian Colonel John Birch, and Charles Clifford, of a Royalist family, had fallen in love. They took refuge with Sir Harry Lingen at Goodrich Castle. But Colonel Birch came and lay siege to the castle, and Sir Harry warned the pair that his small band could not hold out for long.

Taking advantage of a storm, they tried to get across the river to safety, but their horse could not get through the torrent the river had now become and all three were swept away.

Goodrich Castle, haunted by dead lovers. (© David Phelps, 2011)

On stormy nights, if you stand at the riverbank near the castle, you will hear the neighing of the horse and the cries of the lovers as they are parted. Some have even seen a horseman, with a woman behind him, vainly urging his steed to cross the river.

HAMPTON BISHOP

When there was more traffic on the River Wye than there is now, boatmen took great care to be nowhere near the stretch of the river here because, at eight o'clock every evening, a woman in a small boat could be seen travelling along it. This was no ordinary craft, nor did it have a human passenger; the boat travelled faster than any normal sailing vessel, even in dead calm and even against the wind. Those who had witnessed it said that the boat would land on the eastern bank of the river, where the figure would remain for some time, crying in such a dreadful manner that it would almost tear the soul out of your body. Then it would get back in the boat and sail back upstream with equal rapidity, until disappearing suddenly at a spot about half a mile outside the city, where the current is particularly treacherous. This part of the river became known as the Spectre's Voyage and people did well to shun it because, if you saw the figure, your days on this earth could be counted on the fingers of one hand.

Some say that this is the ghost of Isobel Chandos, daughter of the castellan of Hereford, Sir John Chandos. His lord, Humphrey de Bohun, Earl of Hereford, rebelled against Edward II and had Edward's favourite, Piers Gaveston, killed, the actual deed being done by two Welshmen employed by Chandos. Edward bided his time and then, when he felt strong enough, attacked Humphrey and defeated him at the Battle of Boroughbridge. Humphrey was killed in the battle and, although Sir John Chandos had not been present, Edward was still vengeful and sent his followers to kill him. He was dragged onto a boat and Isobel was forced along as well. When they reached Hampton Bishop they landed, and Chandos was beheaded. The sight drove Isobel mad, hence her ghostly wanderings.

Another story has it that Isobel was in love with another of Edward's favourites, Sir Hugh Despencer. Despencer tried to intervene and save the father of the woman he loved but failed and Isobel's heart was broken. Whatever the truth of it, when Roger Mortimer deposed Edward II, he had Despencer hanged in the High Town at Hereford.

HENTLAND

Herefordshire is noted for its high banks and hedges, and there are some good examples of these near this quiet village. One evening in 1953, a man was cycling along one of these lanes near the church when, swinging round a sharp bend, he was confronted with the figure of a woman in the middle of the road. He shut his eyes and pulled hard at his brakes, but also braced himself for the inevitable collision. Yet, when he came to a halt and opened his eyes, he was alone in the lane. Barely a second had gone by and, with the high bank and hedge, there was nowhere that the woman could have gone so quickly. Telling his story later, he was shocked to hear about the Grey Lady, a spectral figure of a woman in a grey cloak, that haunts the area. Some believe she was a nun, from the chapel of Aconbury nunnery that stood here in the Middle Ages; others, more romantically inclined, believe she is the sad ghost of a jilted lover.

HOARWITHY

In the middle of the nineteenth century, a farm labourer called Tom Reece was walking home from Ross. It was just before Christmas and he had enjoyed a good evening. Walking down the lane, he suddenly had the feeling that there was something behind him. He turned to look and saw a big black dog. Tom knew enough about dogs to keep still and let the creature get past him, but the dog just sat down and watched him. When Tom walked on the dog also continued, remaining a few paces behind him.

Tom soon got tired of this and, turning, shouted at it to be off, but the dog took no notice. He threw a stick at it but the dog just let it bounce off him. So Tom took hold of a fallen branch from the hedgerow and advanced on the dog. Now the dog jumped back and rose onto its hind legs. In the moonlight, Tom saw it change into a human form, one that he recognised – that of his own dead father.

Tom fled and got home safely. He could not bring himself to tell anyone about the dog but people noticed that he was getting steadily more withdrawn and depressed. Then, one night, he got up and turned to his brother, who slept in the same bed. 'I've got to go out. Don't worry about me,' he said.

Tom went to a local wood, where he met the dog and followed it further into the woodland. At a specific spot, the dog turned into the figure of his father again. The man pointed to a patch of ground. 'Dig!' it commanded; and Tom did, as best he could. Eventually he unearthed an old leather satchel. 'Throw it in the river!' commanded the ghost, and Tom set out to the Wye and flung the satchel into it.

As soon as the bag had sunk beneath the black water, the ghostly figure disappeared and Tom fainted. When he woke up it was morning and he was chilled to the bone, but his spirits were lifted and he went home with a song on his lips. He never saw the dog or his father again.

There was a pool near the village that had a bad reputation. Teams of horses going past it at night used to shy and become uncontrollable. At least one carter had his leg broken. The pool was said to be at the junction of Hereford Road and Bierless Road. This road is now lost but local historian Heather Hurley believed that it was a corpse way, leading to a burial ground outside the churchyard where the bodies of suicides were interred.

Some say that King Arthur himself was a Hereford man and his ghost has been spotted just south of the village, riding with his bodyguard as if on a hunting expedition. It was just such a sighting that inspired local historian Mary Andere to research Arthurian links to the county.

Hoarwithy seems to be quite a haunted place; the village street is haunted by a lady in white, who has also been seen down by the bridge. Local people maintain that this is the ghost of a nineteenth-century school teacher who was unlucky in love. The fact that she is seen by a bridge, the site of many female suicides in that era, indicates that her story did not have a happy ending.

HOLME LACY

The house, the largest mansion in Herefordshire, is now an 'adults only' hotel. After it passed out of the hands of the Scudamore family in the early part of the twentieth century, it was used as a mental hospital. Staff reported sightings of a Grey

Wye near Hoarwithy, where King Arthur has been seen. (© David Phelps, 2011)

Lady walking about the wards and, even now, several guests have been disturbed by similar sightings, mostly in the gallery.

HOPE UNDER DINMORE

My grandmother, who lived in nearby Bodenham, knew a story of a man forced to run from Hampton Court near London to the Hampton Court in this parish while chased by bloodhounds. He almost made it, but was caught and killed just by the gatehouse. I have not been able to verify the story but the house and grounds are haunted by at least one phantom dog.

There are hounds in a portrait painted of one of the Coningsbys, the family who formerly owned the house. When they were forced to sell up at the beginning of the nineteenth century and pass the house to the Arkwrights, who had made their money in industry, they left the portrait behind, as it was said to be bad luck to the owner of the castle if it was ever removed. The painting is still there.

John Aubrey, the seventeenth-century antiquarian with Herefordshire connections, tells this story: Mr Brown, brother-in-law to the Lord Coningsby, warned several people of his own murder. His phantom appeared to his sister and her maid in Fleet Street, about the time that he was killed in Herefordshire.

KENCHESTER

Here was the Roman settlement of Magnis, now a field. It was built just below the site of the mighty Iron Age 'fort' of Credenhill and probably served as a sub-regional centre for the Dobunni tribe, who were generally quite welcoming to the Roman invaders. Inevitably, there have been reports of a column of Roman soldiers marching

Hampton Court, haunted by a phantom dog. (© David Phelps, 2011)

Kenchester. These quiet fields were once a busy Roman town. (© David Phelps, 2011)

ture by moving between the three houses. Naturally, the National Trust property Croft Castle also claims to have Owen's ghost. Some also claim that an old and mysterious man who is often seen wandering around western Herefordshire is the source for Jackie Kent, the Herefordshire trickster, stories. Others say that Jackie, or Jack o'Kent, was a wizard who had sold his soul to the Devil in return for supernatural powers. But, when he died, the Devil was to have his soul, whether he be buried outside a church or in it. When he died at Kentchurch, he asked to be buried in the church wall there, so that he was neither in the church nor out of it. He asked that his liver and lights (lungs) should be placed on three iron spikes on the church tower and that a dove and a raven would come and fight for them. If the dove won he was heading for heaven, if the raven won then he was heading for hell. Sadly the story does not relate which of them won.

Despite the huge reward offered for his capture, Owen was never betrayed. Some say he died on one of his many wanderings around these hills and is buried in a secret place that few know, which will only be divulged when his principality is in a position to give him a permanent resting place befitting his rank.

The white face of a lady is sometimes glimpsed at a window by people outside the hall. Romantics believe that this is the face of Owen's daughter, vainly waiting for him to return after he set out on his final journey.

The bridge here over the Monnow towards Grosmont was reputedly built by Jackie Kent, but what he built by night fell down in the day as long as the bridge remained incomplete. So Jackie enlisted the help of his master the Devil, on the under-

along the Roman road here, and indeed this would have been a common sight 2,000 years ago as the road was an important communication route between the garrisons of Caerleon and Chester.

KENTCHURCH

A bedroom in Kentchurch Court is said to be haunted by the ghost of Owen Glendower (also spelt Glyndwr), who almost freed Wales from English rule at the beginning of the fifteenth century. After the failure of his rebellion, Owen disappeared and, despite a high price on his head, was never captured.

Three of his daughters were married to English lords who held Kentchurch, Croft Castle and Monnington Court, so it is widely assumed that Owen evaded cap-

Monnow Bridge, built by Jackie Kent and the Devil. (© David Phelps, 2011)

standing that he was to have the first living thing that walked over the bridge. But, as dawn broke and the bridge was finished, Jackie threw a bone across and a poor mongrel dog ran after it – and that was the only reward the Devil received for all his hard work. Another story goes that a local councillor, anxious to take credit for other men's work, was the first over and the prize for the Devil, but that might be a more modern invention. However, richly dressed figures have been seen dancing over the bridge, and as to whether these are the politician and his cronies or just fairies going about their usual business, local opinion is divided.

Cole's Tump, which inspired author M.R. James. (© David Phelps, 2011)

KILPECK

The horror writer M.R. James was a regular visitor to this village between 1906 and 1929 when his god daughter lived here. His story 'A View from a Hill', about a young man who borrows an old of pair of binoculars and starts seeing events from the past through them, is thought to have been inspired by the landscape around the nearby hill Cole's Tump which, even not knowing the story, has a mysterious atmosphere about it.

KINGSLAND

Local stories suggest that the church was originally built at nearby Lawton, but the Devil pulled down the work every night and, in the end, it was decided to move the church to where we see it now, in the village.

KINGTON

Hergest Court, just outside Kington, was where the Red Book of Hergest was found, which Lady Charlotte Guest used as the basis for the Mabinogion. It has a rather gloomy, almost sinister look. In the mid-1980s, my wife and I were walking along the road near it late at night, heading towards a cottage we had rented, when a local farmer stopped his car and insisted on giving us a lift. It was only later I found out why – the sinister reputation of the Court.

Thomas Vaughan was killed at the Battle of Banbury in 1469 and his body was brought back to be buried in Kington church, but his spirit was not of the kind that rested easily in its grave. He reappeared as a fly that tormented cart horses and made them bolt, and even as a black bull that entered Kington church and terrified the congregation. The prosperity of

Hergest Court, home of Black Vaughan. (© David Phelps, 2011)

the town was suffering, so twelve canons from Hereford Cathedral went to Hergest Court to exorcise him. Here he appeared as a huge black dog and, such was his power, that he almost extinguished their candles; but the oldest and least sober of the canons kept his alight and they were able to confine Thomas Vaughan's spirit to a silver box and bury him in the bottom of Hergest Pool.

However, when the head of the Vaughan family is about to die, a huge black dog is said to appear on the lawn outside the Court and howl. The hound was supposed to haunt an upper room in the house and many tenants reported hearing its chains clanking.

There was an oak tree near Hergest which had two blackened footprints under it. This was said to be the spot where Thomas Vaughan had often stood in life to survey his domain. When the oak tree was cut down the footprints disappeared, but the man who chopped down the tree went mad soon afterwards.

Vaughan's wife, who lies so tranquilly beside him in the church, seems to have been a fitting mate for such a tempestuous spirit. Ellen Gethin was of a noble Welsh family. Her beloved brother, David, was killed by their cousin, John Hir. Determined to exact vengeance for the death, she disguised herself as a man and entered a local archery contest. After John Hir had taken his shot, Ellen, taking her turn, raised her bow but turned and killed John Hir, escaping in the resultant confusion. Perhaps that was why she was known as Ellen the Terrible.

There was a tailor who lived in Kington who was terribly addicted to cursing and swearing. One day, a man dressed in black came into his shop and asked to be measured for a suit of clothes. Muttering under

Black Vaughan and Ellen The Terrible – now sleeping peacefully. (© David Phelps, 2011)

his breath, the tailor commenced his task. Everything was fine until he came to the man's feet. Here, instead of the usual boots, were two cloven hooves. Now the tailor realised what his swearing had brought him to. This was either the Devil or the ghost of Black Vaughan come to claim him. He completed his measurements as best he could, and the figure in black appointed a time when he would return to claim the clothes.

The tailor ran to the parson and told him what had happened, promising to mend his ways if the parson could get him out of this fix. On the appointed time, the parson hid behind the counter, and started to pray hard when the figure in black came into the shop. He examined the cloth and expressed himself satisfied, taking out a purse of money, but the parson had warned the tailor that on no account must he take any payment from the Devil. So it began, the Devil cajoling and the parson praying, and the poor old tailor caught between the two of them until the sky grew dark. All through the night it continued until the tailor thought he would go mad – but then the first hint of dawn appeared in the sky and the cock crowed. Then the Devil let out an imprecation that even the tailor had not heard before and disappeared. After this there was one thing for certain; the tailor never cursed nor swore again.

The Stanner Stones, just outside the town, has a spot called the Devil's Garden, on which nothing will ever grow.

KNILL

Walter Map, born in Herefordshire in around 1140, became a courtier of Henry II. He had an illustrious career but is now mostly remembered for his book *De Nugis Curialium: Courtiers' Trifles*, including gossip, anecdotes and accounts of marvellous happenings that members of the royal household might find amusing. Much of this work is devoted to supernatural stories and his work shows a heavy Celtic influence, with the belief in a parallel world that can interact with our own. No wonder then that the standard translation from Walter's Latin into English was carried out by the antiquarian and ghost writer M.R. James.

This is one of those stories. Sir John Knill, whose family had controlled the manor of that name on the Welsh border since the Conquest, married a noble and well-born lady. They were very happy and she soon gave birth to a child. But, on the morning after its birth, the child was found in its cradle with its throat cut. This was bad enough, but the same thing happened to a second and then a third child, despite a careful watch put on them.

Therefore, Sir John and his lady waited fearfully when it was time for their fourth child to be born. There were many fasts, alms and prayers. When the child, a boy, was eventually born, its cradle was placed in the hall, lights were brought and the whole household kept watch.

As the hours of darkness descended, their vigil was interrupted by the arrival of a stranger, weary from a long journey. Sir John did not hesitate but offered the man all the hospitality he could. In return, the stranger joined the household in their watch. As the time passed the man noticed that, despite all their efforts, one by one, all in the hall were falling asleep; all but himself, who now alone maintained the vigil.

At the darkest point of the night he saw an old woman enter the hall and approach the cradle, seizing hold of the child as if to cut its throat. Before she could do so he jumped forward and grabbed hold of her.

The ensuing scuffle awoke the rest of the company, many of whom recognised the women as a respectable and noble woman of the city of Hereford. Sir John and his men threatened and pleaded with her but she would not say a word to them nor explain why she was there.

All the while the stranger kept fast hold of her, despite even the father of the child asking him, for pity's sake, to let her go.

'I will not, because she is not what you think she is but a demon, a ghost that is inhabiting what appears to be a human body,' he replied, and asked Sir John to get one of his retainers to fetch the key of Knill church so he could prove the matter to be so.

The key was brought and the stranger placed the key on the old woman's face. She let out a piercing scream that horrified all who heard it and there, on her face, was the mark of the key as if she had been branded with it.

Now the stranger ordered that the woman whom she resembled be brought to him and, although this took a couple of days, he held tight fast to the creature the whole time. When the old woman arrived it was found that she too had the mark of the key on her face but could not account for it.

Sir John drew his sword to dispatch her, convinced that she was responsible for the deaths of his children, but the man stopped him with a glance. He said:

It is my opinion that the woman who has just been brought here is both virtuous and beloved of God. By her good deeds she has provoked the envy of demons, just as the love of Sir John and his lady have done. This base creature that I hold has been moulded in the likeness of the good woman so as to cast the disgrace of wicked deeds upon her noble soul. But have faith and see what happens when I release it.

Whereupon he let go of the creature, who flew away through the window with a terrible shriek.

After that there were Knills living at Knill Court right up to the Second World War. My grandmother, who was a storyteller and lived at nearby Presteigne, once told me the sad story of the last of that name to live at the Court, Captain Knill, which provides a coda to the above story.

Captain Knill and his wife were very happy but, after the birth of their first and only child, Mrs Knill would not let her husband approach her 'for that sort of thing' (in the euphemistic words of my grandmother, who was born in Victorian times).

Captain Knill took it badly and assuaged the pain with the company of alcohol and prostitutes. Eventually the couple separated and Captain Knill went to live in London, where there was a more plentiful supply of the things to which he was now addicted. This was only discovered one evening in the Blitz when a former footman at the Court who had joined the Metropolitan Police was sent to a run-down house on his beat which had not properly observed the black-out. The door was opened by Captain Knill, looking the worse for wear. Both men recognised each other but, with the tact that was common in that time, neither man let it be known to the other that he had done so. Captain Knill promised to address the problem of the black-out and closed the door — and that was the last that the people of Herefordshire heard about him.

LEA

If a village has got a place called Cut Throat Lane in it you can be sure that dark deeds were carried out there at one time. However, the reason this lane just outside the village got such a frightening name may be due to physics rather than the paranormal.

People reported hearing the sound of a coach and horses coming down the lane yet there has been nothing there. It did not take long for the assumption to be made that some evil adventure had taken place at the spot. Before long, murder was speculated and the road got its name.

It was noted that the ghostly coach was only heard on a cold winter morning when there was frost on the ground, and then only when the sun had recently risen and was beginning to warm the earth. People assumed that whatever crime had been committed there happened on such a morning. It was only in the twentieth century that another explanation presented itself. Someone skilled in physics put the clues together and suggested that the warming sun, striking some feature on the lane and causing the heated air to rush out of a confined space, was making a sound that people misinterpreted as the sound of a coach. What the truth is I do not know, but it would still take a brave soul to wait in that lane in the dark one winter morning, watching for the dawn and listening to the silence, awaiting the sound of the phantom coach.

The Crown Inn is said to have two ghosts. One, that of a woman in a long, flowing gown, haunts the upstairs while the other, a man, haunts the restaurant. The woman creates an uneasy feeling, which means the area she frequents is rarely visited, but the man, an elderly chap, appears quite benign and only gets upset when anyone sits in his favourite seat, probably just as he did when he was alive and was a regular visitor to the bar.

LEDBURY

A modern sighting of a wraith, the appearance of one who has just died, occurred

The Crown Inn – with two very different ghosts. (© David Phelps, 2011)

in the town in 1950. The composer Jack Moeran is little-known these days but, in the middle of the last century, he was ranked alongside Butterworth and Warlock as one of the leaders of the English lyrical movement. He lived in Kington but also spent time here, where his brother was rector.

A friend of his spotted him walking down the High Street and was going to cross the road to speak to him; she had heard he was in Ireland and wanted to know how the trip had gone. But he held up his hand to her, a familiar gesture when he was caught up with some music and did not want to talk. She turned away, a little offended. A few days later she was told the news that Jack had died in Ireland – at the very minute that she had seen him walking in the High Street.

LEOMINSTER

A house in South Street is haunted by the ghost of a highwayman, who has been seen walking down the stairs and through a wall at the bottom which was once a door.

In West Street, the Talbot Hotel was built at a crossroads called the Iron Cross. This was where public executions took place in the town. Probably the most famous victim was a Catholic priest, Roger Cadwallader, executed in 1610. Roger was a native of Stretton Sugwas and from a Catholic family. He had taken holy orders and returned to his native county, but this time, only shortly after the Gunpowder Plot, was a dangerous time for a priest. He was captured, tried and found guilty of treason. He now faced the agonisingly slow death of hanging, drawing and quartering, his head stuck on a spike on top of the Lugg Bridge. It is said that the practice of putting ornamental stone balls on entrance gate-

Ledbury High Street, scene of a modern wraith. (© David Phelps, 2011)

Talbot Hotel and the Iron Cross crossroads. (© David Phelps, 2011)

ways dates from this time. Lords frequently placed the heads of their enemies at their gates as a warning. But in Tudor times, as the supply of heads began to diminish, the practice of replacing them with these stone ornaments developed instead.

The hotel was built some fifty years later but visitors have reported seeing a dark figure dressed in a cloak; people who know this story think it is the ghost of the martyr. However, others say that, since these are licensed premises, it is more likely to be the spirit of William of Wycombe, noted as the composer of the early English lyric 'Sumer is icumin in'. He was exiled to the monastery in Leominster for licentiousness but did not mend his ways and was excommunicated.

Catholics were not always the victims. During the earlier reign of Bloody Mary, a group of Catholic townspeople attacked some Protestants camped at Cursneh Hill, massacring them. For this act, the town was granted its first charter. The site is now an allotment and some of the holders have reported something eerie about the place, and are disinclined to be the last to leave in the evening.

LITTLE BIRCH

In the days before piped water could be taken for granted, good, sweet water was very much prized. It was generally agreed that the best water in the Little Birch area was on the land owned by a farmer called Higgins.

However, he became annoyed by all the trespassers passing over his land and so blocked the spring up. He was smoking a pipe in his kitchen, feeling good about things, when he felt water at his feet. Rushing out he saw a mist by the spring, which took on the shape of a White Lady. Realising that he had upset the spirit of the spring, he rushed to repair the damage, although he was careful to make the new outlet at the foot of his land. This place is still called Higgins Well and can be found on the path from Aconbury to Little Birch.

Higgin's Well – still providing sweet water. (© David Phelps, 2011)

LONGTOWN

The mist can come down very suddenly in the hills up above the town, catching out unwary walkers. One such, at the end of the nineteenth century, found himself caught in a sudden fog and stood still for a long time, uncertain of the way. Then a figure came out of the mist, wearing a broad-brimmed hat and a cloak. He did not speak but beckoned to the man, who soon recognised that he had returned to the right path. Turning to thank his guide, he found himself alone. Recounting the story to friends later on and describing the man who had saved him, one of them cried, 'Why that was old Tom Hutton! He's been dead these two years.'

But not all guides are helpful. Whatever you do, do not follow a large black crow that sometimes appears to lost walkers, for this is the Devil and he will lead you astray, as will the figure of a lady dressed in black, who has a liking for luring travellers towards long drops on the Black Mountains.

There is a story that, years ago, on the hills above Longtown, there lived a hired shepherd, who managed a little farm for his master. On either side of the farm was the land of two brothers, farming for their father. This was a time when all the sheep ran together and there was terrible jealousy and animosity between the shepherds in consequence, but a good shepherd knew their sheep. If they whistled, theirs would come to them.

The brothers hated the hired man because he was a good shepherd and they were not. At last, they found him alone on the mountain one day and told him they would murder him. There was no one about to help him.

'If you kill me the very crows will cry out and speak it,' said the shepherd, but they murdered him anyway and hid his body.

The body was eventually discovered but there was no evidence to show who the murderers were. However, crows took to whirling round the heads of the two

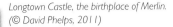
Longtown Castle, the birthplace of Merlin.
(© David Phelps, 2011)

covered. Sometimes a story is so good that it travels.

To the east of Longtown Castle there is a mound called Mynydd Fyrddyn, which can be translated as either 'sloping mountain' or 'Merlin's mountain'. Tradition has it that this is the burial place of the great wizard himself.

Back in the nineteenth century, a Baptist minister preached a sermon against superstition and belief in such things as ghosts. One of the congregation was afterwards heard to say:

I know what I have seen, I helped myself to turn a man in his grave, up at Capel-y-fin; he came back, and we thought to stop him, but after we turned him he came back seven times worse. He was a hurdle maker, and you could hear him tap, tap, tap, chopping wood for his hurdles all about the place where he used to work. No use that preacher telling me there's no ghosts!

brothers all day long. Nothing they did could scare the crows off and they started to fear that these crows were the spirit of the shepherd come to haunt them. When they could bear it no longer, one said to the other, 'Brother, do you remember when we killed the poor shepherd on the mountain top there? He said that the very crows would cry out against us.'

These words were overheard by a man in the next field; the matter was looked into and eventually the brothers were both hanged for the murder.

This is a good story but classical scholars might recall the Greek myth of the poet Ibycus who was killed by robbers. As he was dying he called out to a flock of cranes to avenge him. The cranes hovered over the theatre in Corinth, where the murderers were, until one called out, 'Behold, the avengers of Ibycus!' So was the murder dis-

LYONSHALL

Like many Herefordshire villages, this one was once connected to the wide world by a railway branch line but, regrettably, it can now only be accessed by road. However, the old railway station can still be identified and, if locals are to be believed, one of the railway employees is also still around. He takes the form of an old man, looking rather sad and down on his luck, and is reported to be the 'fetch' of a former long-serving porter who cannot quite believe that there are no more passengers to be

Castle Farm, site of treasure. (© David Phelps, 2011)

helped. He can occasionally be seen walking along the road outside the old station.

MADLEY

Castle Farm and the stretch of nearby road is haunted by the figure of a man, locally assumed to be the guardian of treasure found at the farm at the beginning of the nineteenth century. Why the guardian is still haunting the place after the discovery of the hoard has not been determined, but it is thought that the gold is linked to a reputed tunnel that runs from the farm to the church, so perhaps it was church gold and the spectre wants it returned to the rightful owners.

MARDEN

Some 1,500 years ago, the bell of the church was lost in the river and locals believed it had been taken by the spirit of the river,

although another explanation was that it was taken by the ghost of a poor drowned woman whose body had been recently discovered. In consultation with a cunning man who knew about such things, the locals devised a plan to rescue the bell. A team of twelve white freemartins (heifers) was obtained and attached to the bell with yokes of yew and bands of rowan, another sacred tree. The bell was then drawn out in perfect silence. But, just as the bell was coming out of the river, one of the drivers called out, 'In spite of all the devils in hell, now we'll land Marden's great bell!' Immediately the bell fell back into the river and the spirit's voice was heard, 'If it had not been for your rowan bands and your yew tree pin I'd have had your twelve freemartins in.'

That this story, like so many oral traditions, had some basis in truth was discovered in 1848 when a pool by the river was cleaned out and an old bronze bell, of the kind used by the Celtic church, was found under the silt. This bell can now be seen in Hereford Museum.

St Ethelbert's
*Well, where the saint was first
buried. (© David Phelps, 2011)*

Nearby Sutton Walls is reputedly the site of a royal hall used by King Offa of Mercia, although no archaeology has been yet found to confirm this. It was here that Offa is supposed to have murdered his rival, Ethelbert, King of East Anglia, and secreted the body in the marshy ground near what is now the village of Marden. But the body was discovered, thanks to a miraculous glow that came from the spot. The body was given a proper burial in the monastery in Hereford and, when it was removed, a spring broke forth from the spot. This can now be seen inside the church.

MIDDLETON ON THE HILL

Gravenor's Bridge is haunted by a female figure in white, who drifts across the bridge on certain moonlit nights. Her story is lost but many local people believe that she is the spirit of some local girl unlucky in love, who may have ended her earthly sufferings at this spot but whose ethereal remains are still tied to it.

MORDIFORD

The nearby Haugh (pronounced Hoff) Wood was haunted by a dragon. It had been found in the wood by a local girl when it was small. She took it home as a pet, but it soon outgrew the pig pen where she had confined it and ended up eating her family's sheep and then her family and then her. So terrible were its depredations that a Hereford man agreed to kill it. The dragon was in the habit of coming down Serpent Lane towards the confluence of the Lugg and the Wye to drink. The man hid in a barrel at the spot and shot the dragon with a crossbow. Unfortunately, the dragon's final breath was so poisonous that it killed him as well.

Up to the beginning of the nineteenth century, a green dragon was painted on the outside of Mordiford church, but was removed by a superstitious vicar after a terrible flood that local people said was the dragon's revenge.

Some people say that the village name comes from Mordred's ford and that his banner was a green dragon, but how they know that I have no idea.

MUCH MARCLE

Hellens, the large house here, was owned by the Walwyn family. In the eighteenth century, the youngest daughter of the house, Hetty, fell in love with one of the grooms.

Haugh Wood, haunt of a dragon. (© David Phelps, 2011)

Since he was only the son of a local farmer, the boy was sacked as soon as Mr Walwyn got word of it and Hetty was forbidden to see him again.

But, using the confusion caused by the preparations for Christmas as cover, they eloped and nothing was heard from them for five years. Then Hetty returned, alone and in rags – but this was not the usual tale of love gone wrong. They had been happy and successful in their new home in America, but her husband had died and she had been cheated by his business partners. She still had her large diamond ring, the only thing left of her love. Mr Walwyn might have thrown her out of doors, but she was his daughter so he allowed her to stay on the condition that she never left her room, in case she met another unsuitable man. A bell was put up on the roof with the rope going down to her bedroom, so that she could summon a servant. Even after his death, while she was given greater liberty, she never left the house again. After her death, people looking up to her bedroom still saw a sad white face looking out of the window and the bell, which is still there, will occasionally ring – although the rope has been disconnected. In the Second World War, a young officer staying at the house came down to breakfast one morning complaining of being woken up in the middle of the night by an old woman in a dressing gown. There was no one of that description staying in the house and the young man had been given Hetty's room to sleep in.

Another room is haunted by the ghost of a priest. In the Civil War, the Walwyns were Royalist but nearby Gloucester was strictly in favour of Parliament. A troop of Roundhead cavalry from that city was

Hellens, with the bell tower on the left of the roof. (© David Phelps, 2011)

camped at Much Marcle church and heard of the Walwyns; they decided to teach them a lesson. As they rode down the drive, they spotted a priest and chased him into the house and into a room where they killed him. There is still something eerie about that room and many people report feeling uneasy in it.

ORCOP

There will always be nine witches from the bottom of Orcop to the end of Garway Hill as long as water runs.

On the north side of Orcop Hill is a place called The Devil's Wood, where some believe human sacrifice has been carried out since before Christianity arrived here. If the wood was ever to be felled, the owner would die within the year. Sensitive people who know that story say they feel a sense of dread in the wood, as if the spirits of those sacrifices still haunt it.

ORLETON

The pub, the Boot, is haunted by a phantom piano that plays in the middle of the night when the pub is shut. Some of the regulars will tell you that this is the ghost of a former barman who had a dispute with the landlord. The quarrel was so bitter that he was painted out of a picture of the staff that hung in the bar – as if he never existed. But, in revenge, he is still making his presence felt.

Orleton churchyard – where the resurrection will begin. (© David Phelps, 2011)

PEMBRIDGE

Dr Breton was the minister here in Cromwell's time. He had married the daughter of a rich local family, but his wife had been troubled that the wealth had been accumulated by taking church land that had formerly been used to help the poor.

Soon after her death she appeared to her maidservant, and made the girl come with her to fields now owned by her brother. 'Observe how much of this field I measure with my feet. All this belongs to the poor, it being gotten from them by unlawful means,' it said. The girl did so and then went to the brother and told him what she had seen. Deeply affected, he made sure that the income from that land went towards charitable purposes.

Strictly speaking this place should be called New Pembridge. The original Pembridge was a place of great wickedness. The vicar of Pembridge got so fed up with his flock that he warned them that, if they did not mend their ways, the very earth would swallow them up. They just laughed at him and, in disgust, the vicar left the village. Undaunted, the villagers held a dance to celebrate and one of the musicians was a fiddler from Eardisland. After the dance was over he set off home but, as soon as he reached his cottage, he remembered that he had left a pair of fine white gloves behind, tied with red ribbons, his fee for playing that night. These were too good to lose so he set off back to Pembridge. But when he got there the village had totally disappeared, having been swallowed up by Shobdon marshes. All that was left was

Pembridge Market Hall. This replaced the market hall which drowned in the marshes. (© David Phelps, 2011)

a well which, folk say, if you drop a stone into, you will hear it strike the top of the old church steeple.

So it is understandable that the inn here is called the New Inn, though the name actually refers to it having served as a farmhouse and courthouse before it took on its current purpose. As befits such an old building, there are at least two ghosts here. One, that of a young lady in a long gown, is the daughter of a local farmer and she haunts the upstairs. The story goes that her lover went off to find fame and fortune, and finding these two has always meant leaving the county. He never returned and now she haunts this spot, although she only appears to women, as if to tell them of her sad fate. Downstairs, meanwhile, is haunted by the ghost of a soldier, a redcoat. Some think that this is the ghost of the young lady's

lover but, if so, it is particularly tragic that the two never meet, although separated by only a few feet.

PENCOMBE

By the mid part of the nineteenth century, many of the medieval churches of Herefordshire had fallen into a state of disrepair and an extensive programme of re-building and re-modelling took place, with what might be called mixed results. In the village of Pencombe, the church was some distance from the site of the village and the decision was taken to pull the old one down and rebuild nearer people's houses. This might have pleased the living but the dead, buried in the old graveyard, were not so happy. Soon reports came that

Pengethley Manor, haunted by a little girl and an old lady.

Peterchurch. Somewhere here a treasure is hidden. (© David Phelps, 2011)

their ghosts could be seen in the old grave-yard, some even venturing up Church Lane towards the village. It was quickly decided to keep the church where it was, and merely repair it. Since then the churchyard and Church Lane have been quiet.

PENGETHLEY

The manor is now a hotel but, when it was a private residence back in 1816, it burnt down, killing a young girl called Harriet. She is still seen by staff and the occasional guest. The ruins of the old manor are also reported to be haunted by an old lady who sometimes walks in the reception area and library, wearing a long, black dress.

PETERCHURCH

The old manor of Snodhill was built by the Prosser family at the Restoration. When a death is about to occur in this family, a ghostly procession, complete with torches, proceeds down the lane outside the manor. At its head is a priest walking without looking to left or right, and behind him a horse-drawn hearse with a coffin inside. At the same time, a White Lady is often seen walking in the grounds. In the park of the house lies buried, by popular belief, a vast treasure, said to lie 'no deeper than a hen can scratch'.

Perhaps this is true because, at the Golden Well in Peterchurch, a man once caught a fish that had a gold chain around its neck. A sculpture of the fish can be seen in the church. Possibly the chain had somehow got separated from the rest of the treasure.

PONTRILAS

River mist can play funny tricks on the senses. People have claimed that they have heard and seen the ghosts of warriors fighting on the riverbank south of the village. The spot was marked by a round mound with a bare path around it on which the grass never grew, where the bodies from the battle are buried. This spot is called Monmouth Cap and people have therefore assumed that this relates to the Monmouth rebellion of 1685, but the fighting then came nowhere near Herefordshire. More likely this is just a memory of one of the innumerable border skirmishes that took place in this area between the English and the Welsh.

A man by the name of Tom Davies once agreed to mow the grass at this place. It was a hot harvest time and he decided to do the mowing at night instead of in the day because of the heat. He was only half-way through his task when he heard music and, looking up, saw a band of soldiers on the mound with a great number of officers and their ladies dancing. Tom dropped his scythe and ran as fast as he could. When he told this story to the people of Pontrilas they just laughed at him and said that it was only the fairies dancing that he had seen; they were always there at that time.

ROSS

The King Charles II Hotel stands in Broad Street. In 1973 someone idly took a photo of the building and the resulting exposure showed a white face staring out from one of the windows. On enquiry, it was not the face of anyone from the hotel nor was anyone in that room when the photo was taken.

When the feat was attempted again thirty years later by a photographer from the local paper, using a digital camera, he found that, no matter how he angled the flash, it always reflected off the window where the ghost was supposed to be, so that all that he was left with was a series of photos with angry red blobs.

Half a mile to the south-east of the town lies Alton Court, owned, in the seventeenth century, by the Markey family. Mr Markey was a hard master, having fired one gardener when a late frost killed some of his best plants. The replacement, a young man called Roger Mortimer, caught the eye of Markey's daughter, Clara.

But Mr Markey had other plans. He was arranging the marriage between Clara and a member of the wealthy Rudhall family. Roger, previously a happy fellow, now started to show signs of distraction and his parents feared that he had been bewitched.

A few days before the marriage was to go ahead, Roger's body was found floating in the Wye near Wilton Bridge. Because it was assumed to be suicide, he was buried at a crossroads with a stake through his heart, at a place then called Corpse Cross but which has now been given the much more tasteful name of Copse Cross Street.

Within a few days of this, Mr Markey was dragging the inconsolable Clara down the

Wilton Bridge, where Roger's body was found. (© David Phelps, 2011)

Old Maid's Walk – where Clara can still occasionally be glimpsed. (© David Phelps, 2011)

aisle of St Mary's Church. But, when she was asked if she took this man as her husband, she let out a terrible shriek and fainted. She was taken home but then disappeared, to be found at Alton Road crossroads looking for the grave of her beloved. She was taken back to the house and locked away but repeatedly she found means of escape, always being found at the same place. Eventually her family had to let her have her way, but her mind never recovered and, into old age, she constantly made that journey to Corpse Cross so that that route became known as Old Maid's Walk.

People who pass by that road still sometimes meet an old lady looking distraught, but she does not answer their offers of help and only leaves behind a feeling of great sadness.

The ghost of an old lady has also been seen in a rowing boat travelling under Wilton Bridge. Most reports suggest she was weeping. Whether this is another sad tale or whether the river also held memories for Clara, I cannot tell.

ST WEONARDS

Those who have glimpsed the ghostly form of a monk in the churchyard might be letting their imaginations run away with them because there was no monastic settlement here and therefore no monks buried in the grounds. However, this figure might be focused on more earthly pursuits as a great treasure is locally believed to be buried in the mysterious mound in the churchyard. Some believe it is St Weonard himself, buried in a golden coffin; others say he is buried on top of a golden chest filled with gold, on top of which are inscribed these words, 'Where this stood is another, twice

St Weonard, buried in a golden coffin. (© David Phelps, 2011)

as good. But where that is no one knows.' This tumulus was opened in 1855 and found to contain ashes and fragments of human bone. Another type of ghost has also been seen here, that of a pig with a saddle on its back. What a pig was doing with a saddle on its back calls for more research, or more speculation.

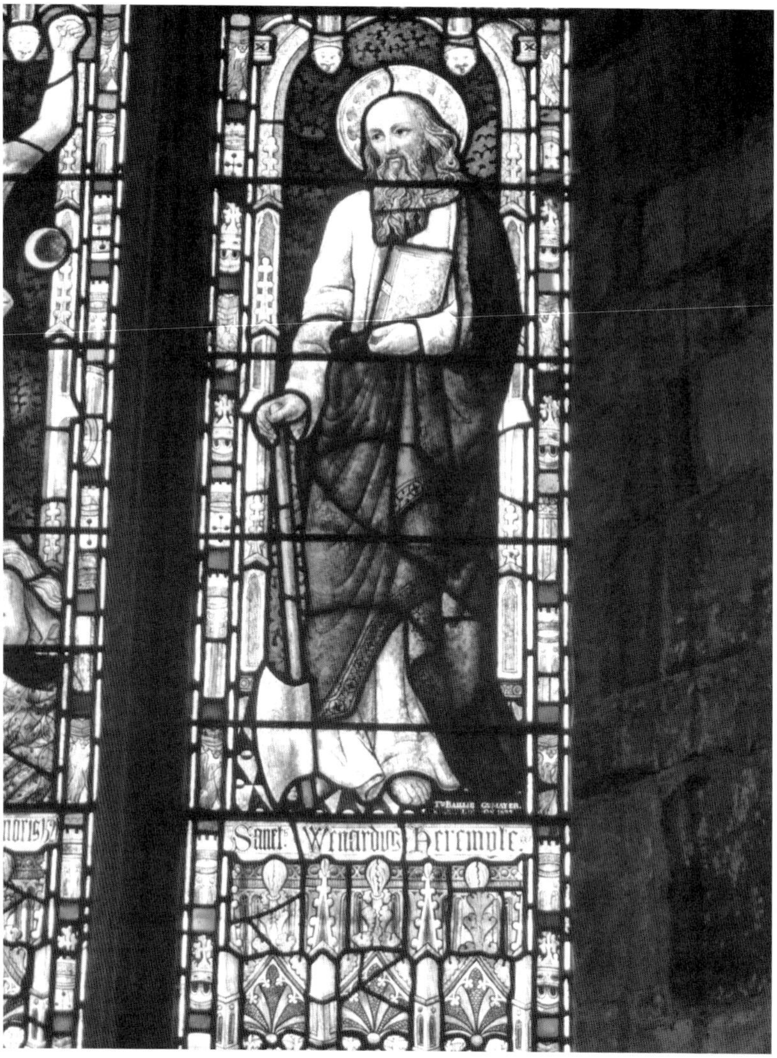

The main road that passes through St Weonards is haunted by the ghost of a sheep stealer. After the enclosures of the eighteenth century, stealing a farmer's sheep, especially from one believed not to treat his workforce fairly, was considered rough natural justice. One such man, needing to feed his family, abducted one of his master's sheep, killed it, and then headed home with it tied to his back. He came to a large stone beside the road and saw it as an opportunity to rest. Laying the sheep on top of it, he sat down to recover, but the sheep overbalanced and fell down the other side, strangling the unfortunate man. It was thus the farmer found him the next morning, as he was looking for his sheep. Since then the spot has been avoided by those

Lough Pool, haunted by a lavender ghost. (© David Phelps, 2011)

in the know, who find something eerie around it.

Oak Apple Day or Royal Oak Day (29 May) used to be called in these parts Shig Shagging Day. Said to commemorate the future Charles II's escape from the Battle of Worcester by hiding in an oak tree (although the battle took place on 3 September 1651), the date is now believed by folklorists to celebrate an older agricultural festival, the significance of which has now been lost. The unusual local name derives from the custom whereby children gathered oak twigs that had galls and leaves attached, which they would place in their hats, and would then visit the more prosperous inhabitants of the village to solicit money. Anyone who refused was rewarded with a chorus in which the refrain 'shig-shag' featured prominently.

SELLACK

The local pub, the Lough Pool, recently closed. Perhaps the new owners do not realise that they are taking on a ghost whose manifestation is the strong smell of lavender. At least they will not need an air freshener.

Shobdon; the old, discarded church. (© David Phelps, 2011)

SHOBDON

Just outside the village is a tumulus called the 'Devil's Shovelful'. The village was once inhabited by a contented and pious population, with one of the best churches in Christendom, so Old Nick decided to destroy the place. He took his shovel, loaded it with a great mound of earth, and set off for Shobdon. Just before he got to the village he ran into the village cobbler, who was so frightened he dropped his bag of old shoes that he was carrying.

'Is this Shobdon?' enquired the prince of darkness. Fortunately the cobbler was a quick thinker. 'No,' he replied. 'I am look-ing for the same place myself and I have worn out all these shoes in the searching. It is not in this direction.'

The Devil dropped his shovel full of earth and went back up the road, muttering to himself, but the people of Shobdon were so fearful that he might return that they tore down their beautiful church and lived a life of wickedness from that day forth.

It is said that, from that time, a cobbler has lived in the house immediately oppo-site the tumulus, and if you don't believe my tale you will find the remains of the old church up on top of the hill where the people left it. If you are there very early in the morning, you might hear the ghostly chuckles of the old cobbler, laughing that he fooled the Devil.

Portway Inn, where a brownie was upset. (© David Phelps, 2011)

STAUNTON ON WYE

If you have ever misplaced your keys, you have probably blamed your poor memory or another member of the household – but there might be a supernatural explanation. When the keys to the Portway Inn went missing at the beginning of the nineteenth century, the inhabitants knew exactly what had happened. They had upset the brownie who lived in the inn and performed some of the chores. The family placed a small cake on the hob as a peace offering and sat in a circle round the hearth with their eyes closed. After a while, the keys were thrown violently against the wall behind the sitters.

The primary school here was formerly a private boarding school, built in the nineteenth century, which might account for why it is a bit larger and more gothic than you would expect. The boarding school was never a success, and does not seem to have been a happy place as a boy is reputed to have hanged himself in the bell tower. On the anniversary of his death, it is said that the bell rope still drips blood. Unfortunately no one can now remember what that date is, so the veracity of the story has not been tested.

STOKE EDITH

At the entrance to the Foley estate the road takes a sharp bend. Some say that the Foleys of old refused to allow the road to go through their land but made it take this diversion. On a regular basis the brick wall here has to be re-built after a motorist fails to take the bend successfully. Most people blame speed but some drivers have felt some dark presence in the car as they

Stoke Edith Bend – the wall after a recent accident. (© David Phelps, 2011)

approach the bend and a pull on the steering wheel, almost as if something is trying to gain control of it.

Back in the eighteenth century a coach, coming home late at night, killed a Tarrington man at this spot and since then the place has had something of a curse about it. The local suspicion is that the ghost of this unfortunate is trying to bring others to their doom.

The big house burnt down in the 1920s. The fire brigade rushed from Hereford but were unable to do anything because their pumps were frozen. Daphne du Maurier used the incident for the destruction of Mandalay in her book *Rebecca*.

The eponymous Edith is St Edith, daughter of King Edgar, who lived in the tenth century. She had no wish to live in the comfort her birth could have given her but wished to live a religious life, so her father made her abbess of Wilton when she was only fifteen years of age. She was deter-

mined to build a church at this fine spot and was so single minded that she helped in the building herself by carrying water from the nearest brook to make the mortar, even though it was quite some distance away. However, she became exhausted by the work and knelt down to pray to God to give her sufficient strength. Instead, a miraculous spring gushed forth at the spot where she knelt and she was able to use that for the work.

STOKE LACY

The stretch of the A465 that runs from the church around the bend and onwards to Bromyard has more than its fair share of motor accidents. Most people blame speed but the motorists involved claim a different version of the story. Similarly to the feeling in Stoke Edith, they say that it felt as if someone had grabbed the steering wheel and tugged it, as if trying to prevent them making the corner. This made local people remember an incident that happened in the 1930s. A car was driving through the village, the couple in it having an argument. One of them – bystanders were not sure which – grabbed the steering wheel, causing the car to crash, killing the woman.

Keen story hunters might note a strange similarity in this tale to that of the 'Hairy Hands' of Dartmoor. The lonely road between Two Bridges and Moretonhampstead was greatly feared by travellers, especially the spot at the bridge over the East Dart near Postbridge. At this point, several motorists have experienced a pair of hairy hands materialise out of nowhere, grab hold of the steering wheel and cause them to crash. There have been several fatalities where no fault could be found with the car, and records of similar events go back several centuries, where drivers of coaches reported the same events.

TEDSTONE DELAMERE

The brook here is connected with a miracle. A farmer had his best mare and foal stolen. The daughter of the farmer, for whom the foal had been an especial favourite, prayed that she might be able to follow the foal's hoof prints. Miraculously they appeared on the road, and the girl and the farm servants were able to follow them without difficulty until they came to the brook, where the hoof prints disappeared. Reasoning that the thief had followed the stream to avoid detection, they examined the banks until they found the foal's prints again, this time marked in solid rock, where they had come out of the stream. They followed the prints further and discovered the thief at the spot called Witchery Hole, or,

some believe, at the Hoarstone. Old time residents of the village may still be able to point out to you the marks made by the foal, or tell you that, if you take a walk by the stream, you can still sometimes hear the splashing of a ghostly foal.

WEOBLEY

It is said that, if you visit the church and walk seven times backwards around each tier of steps on the preaching cross, meanwhile reciting the Lord's Prayer backwards, you will summon up the Devil, and much good may it do you.

In the nineteenth century there was a farm labourer named Tom, who worked at Devereux Wootton Farm but lived at Kinnersley. Each evening for several weeks, as he walked home in the dusk, he met a lady. But he knew better than to talk to her before first being spoken to. Then, one night, he found her sitting on a stile and was forced to ask, 'Please lady, let me pass.'

'Thank you, I have waited years for someone to speak to me.' She then made him return to Devereux Wootton with her. By the time they got there, all the servants seemed to have gone to bed but the doors were wide open and all the rooms lit. They went to the attic where the lady, who said her name was Lady Berrington, opened an oak chest and took out a roll of papers. She gave them to Tom, warning him on no account to read them, but to throw them into a pool near the house.

When he did so, if he heard sweet music, she had made it to heaven but if he heard bad language she was bound for hell. He carried out the task and was relieved to hear the loveliest music he had ever heard. Then he made a mistake. He told the story and it was said that he was never right afterwards.

Weobley Cross, where you can summon the Devil. (© David Phelps, 2011)

Dunwood Farm, also near Weobley, was haunted by the ghost of 'Old Gregg', a farmer who had threatened to disinherit his son and was rewarded by being served stewed toad. He died a slow and painful death and then walked his land as he did in life, as if he refused to believe that he had died.

Farming has always been an uncertain profession. Another farmer committed suicide at Field's End Farm and haunted Garnstone Park in the shape of a calf. He also pulled the bedclothes off sleepers at the farmhouse. He was eventually exorcised and his spirit buried at the bottom of the pool in Garnstone Park.

The old mansion of Garnstone was originally built at the bottom of the hill but, when the workmen returned each day, they found the work they had done the previous day had been undone and the stones carried some distance away. After several days of this, a local cunning man was found who explained that the site that had been chosen was a particular spot beloved by the fairies and it was they who were moving the stones to a place they would accept. So the current site was chosen instead, even though it was higher up the hill and more inconvenient, and the building carried on uninterrupted. Eventually that was demolished and a grander house, Garnstone Castle, was built in its stead, but that too has now gone and the fairies have been left in peace.

Burton Farm, in the late seventeenth century, was troubled by a poltergeist, then generally assumed to be a demon. It would knock on the door, but, when this was opened, no one could be seen. It would upturn the furniture, spoil food, hide bread, sour the milk, cause cattle to die and even demolished a half roast pig.

A valiant Welshman, one John Jones, agreed to watch for the demon one night, armed with a sword, a mastiff dog and a lantern. He had not long got into bed when there was a loud knocking at the door, which burst open; the light went out, the dog started to howl and it felt to Jones that a host of cats had invaded the room, screaming and breaking the window. He was out of that bed faster than he had ever got out before and was half a mile away before anyone could stop him. No inducement could be found to make him return.

Westhide Wood, where the Devil got the friar. (© David Phelps, 2011)

WESTHIDE

Shucknall is, according to some, derived from Shuck's (The Devil's) Hill. How it got that name might be explained by the following story:

Once there was a friar who lived in Westhide Wood. He was not greatly troubled by devotion, but much preferred sport and drinking. One day he heard that there was to be badger baiting at the Bell in Tillington, so he trapped a badger, stuck it in a sack, threw the sack over his shoulder and set off through the wood. He had not gone far when he noticed that the sack was getting heavier, and then a voice called out, 'Mamma calls.' He looked around but could see nothing. He set off again and his sack was getting even heavier, and then he heard another voice, 'Dadda calls.' There was no mistaking the fact that the voice was coming from the sack. He dropped it down and opened it up to take a look inside; out popped the Devil, who seized hold of the friar and took him straight down to hell.

Some have maintained that the ghost of the friar can still be seen here, but walkers in this quiet wood might be calmed by the story having anti-clerical purposes – the strange voices coming from the sack alluding to his parents being a monk and a nun who had conceived the friar sinfully, and had ended up in hell.

WESTON UNDER PENYARD

If you visit Bollitree Castle expecting to see medieval battlements you are in for a disappointment, just as a Spanish princess was back in the eighteenth century.

Thomas Hopkins, the local landowner, went on the Grand Tour, as was expected of a young gentleman in those days. While in Europe, he met and fell in love with a Spanish princess. However, the young lady made it clear that she was quite unprepared to live anywhere apart from a castle. Thomas, who had a perfectly fine seventeenth-century manor house back home in Herefordshire, was in desperation. He ordered that something like a castle should be built back home, plundering stones from the nearby authentically medieval Penyard Castle and a Bristol church.

But the young lady, when she arrived, was not so easily deceived. There must have been a terrible reckoning with the lovelorn young man, and all his efforts and expense was wasted. What happened then is unclear but certainly the Spanish princess was not seen again in those parts. Some say she went back to her family but others told a darker tale.

Whatever the truth of it, the distracted ghost of Thomas Hopkins has been seen wandering miserably in the garden of the house and, more worryingly, the ghost of the young lady has been spotted angrily ascending the stairs.

Local legend has it that Thomas Hopkins would have been better advised looking more closely at the stones of Penyard Castle before he removed them, as there are stories that a great treasure is buried here, guarded by a jackdaw.

Two great barrels full of money are hidden in a subterranean vault but a local farmer determined that they should be his, jackdaw or not. Taking no chances, he brought twenty steers to break down the iron doors of the vault wherein the treasure lay, with harnesses made from yew wood and a rowan wood goad, both woods known to offer protection against dark forces. The cattle succeeded and the farmer, peering in, saw the jackdaw perched on one of the barrels. Thinking that he would soon be richer than any duke or earl, he let

Bollitree Castle, which failed to impress a princess. (© David Phelps, 2011)

out a cry and shouted, 'I believe I shall have it!' The door immediately closed shut with a terrible clang and a voice in the air cried, 'Had it not been for your quicken tree goad and your yew tree pin, you and your cattle had all been drawn in!' He thought better about trying again. (*See* the entry for Marden with which this story, one of many about hidden treasure and secret passages in the county, may have become confused.)

WHITNEY ON WYE

The Rhydspence Inn is haunted by the figure of a woman, popularly supposed to be that of a former landlady who was able to bewitch the cattle of passing drovers so that they could not leave until the drovers had paid for overnight accommodation.

Before the nearby toll bridge was built, the Wye was crossed by a ferry. The ferryman made a decent living but, one day, two labourers down on their luck, became jealous of the man's income, stabbed him to death and stole the jug in which he kept his savings.

With their new riches, they decided to spend the night at the Rhydspence, but, when they tried to sleep, the jug started to clatter about of its own accord. The robbers screamed so loud that the landlord came running to see what the fuss was about.

Wormelow Tump – destroyed by road widening. (© David Phelps, 2011)

He recognised the jug as belonging to the ferryman. Their crime discovered, the men confessed and were hanged.

WORMELOW

Opposite the Tump Inn formerly stood Wormelow Tump, reputed to have been the burial place of Anyr, the son of King Arthur, killed by his father. In a fit of remorse, Arthur ordered a magnificent burial mound to be built, moated by diverting the Gamber Brook. The nearby spring from which the Gamber flows is called the Eye of Anyr. Whether it was because of the water shimmering around it or some other magical properties, it was said that no man could measure it the same twice. Sadly, Herefordshire Council destroyed it in the nineteenth century as part of a road widening scheme.

The Tump Inn itself has been the site of weird events, including a floral scent coming from the ladies' toilet that is so beautiful it cannot come from any air freshener.

WORMSLEY

Always beware if your house is called a grange, because this name, originally just meaning a house with farm buildings attached, seems prone to attracting spectres.

Wormelow Tump Inn – with a ghostly scent in the ladies'. (© David Phelps, 2011)

Such is the case with Wormsley Grange, the forbidding early Georgian house which was the birthplace of Richard Payne Knight, one of the founders of the school of the picturesque, that did much to create the Romantic movement at the end of the eighteenth century. The place is haunted by a beautiful lady dressed in silks and jewels, presumably of the early Georgian period, and a gentleman dressed in black, who haunt the drive at twelve o'clock every night. Fortunately they can only be seen by people who were born around the hour of midnight, that is between 11 p.m. and 1 a.m. With impeccable rural logic, this is given as the reason why so few people have seen them. Their story is not known but is thought to be connected with an indelible stain on the floor of one of the rooms. If they were lovers, you can be sure that their romance did not go smoothly.

YARPOLE

A ghost was laid in the Haugh Pool in this village, confined to a goose quill instead of the usual silver snuff box. If this was an attempt to save money it might not have worked, because there have been reports of a ghostly lady riding a grey horse along the main road through the village, with complete disdain for any motorists driving along it.

Herefordshire – with locations mentioned in the text. (© Marina Phelps, 2011)

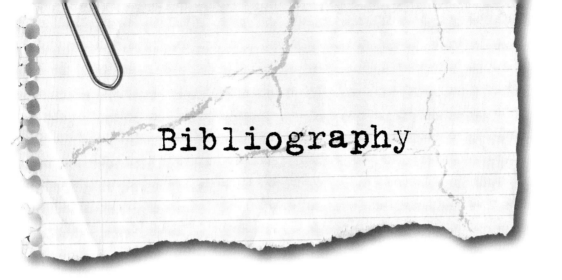

Bibliography

Joynes, Andrew, *Medieval Ghost Stories* (The Boydell Press, 2001)

Leather, Ella Mary, *Folk-Lore of Herefordshire* (Jakeman & Carver, 1912)

Matthews, Rupert, *Haunted Herefordshire* (Logaston Press, 2008)

McCorristine, Shane, *Spectres of the Self* (Cambridge University Press, 2010)

Palmer, Roy, *Herefordshire Folklore* (Logaston Press, 2002)

Trubshaw, Bob, *Explore Folklore* (Heart of Albion Press, 2002)

Other titles published by The History Press

Herefordshire Folk Tales

DAVID PHELPS

For the first time, these enchanting folk tales, the origins of which lie in the oral tradition, have been gathered together in book form. Although on the surface this charming collection may appear quaint, these stories tell of strange happenings in the peaceful Herefordshire countryside, formed from early attempts to explain the natural and spiritual world. From the Saxon king of East Anglia who became the patron saint of Hereford Cathedral, to the story of the black hound of Baskerville Hall which inspired Arthur Conan Doyle, these gripping tales have really stood the test of time.

978 0 7524 4969 2

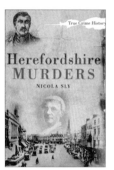

Herefordshire Murders

NICOLA SLY

Herefordshire Murders brings together twenty-eight murderous tales, some which were little known outside the county and others which made national headlines. Herefordshire was home to one of Britain's most infamous murderers, Major Herbert Rowse Armstrong, who, in 1921, poisoned his wife and attempted to poison a fellow solicitor in Hay-on-Wye. However, the county has also experienced many lesser known murders, including the case of two-year-old Walter Frederick Steers, brutally killed in Little Hereford in 1891; and the Jane Haywood, murdered by her husband in 1903.

978 0 7524 5360 6

Herefordshire Pubs

JOHN EISEL & RON SHOESMITH

Illustrated with over 200 old photographs, postcards and promotional advertisements, this absorbing collection offers the reader an insight into the life of many Herefordshire pubs past and present, and highlights some of the changes and events that have taken place during the last century. From the days when the pubs were filled with agricultural workers and gentlemen drinkers to the pool tables and cigarette machines of today's establishments, this book provides a fascinating and comprehensive history of brewing in the county.

978 0 7524 4466 6

Haunted Worcestershire

ANTHONY POULTON-SMITH

This fascinating A-Z tour of the haunted hotspots of Worcestershire contains strange tales of spectral sightings, active poltergeists and restless spirits appearing in streets, inns, churches, estates, public buildings and private homes across the area. This collection of stories, a product of both historical accounts and numerous interviews conducted with local witnesses, is sure to appeal to all those intrigued by Worcestershire's haunted heritage.

978 0 7524 4872 5

Visit our website and discover thousands of other History Press books.

www.thehistorypress.co.uk